WOODWORKING
BASICS

WOODWORKING
BASICS
The principles and skills of good joinery

Alan Goodsell and Randall Maxey

First published 2018 by
Guild of Master Craftsman Publications Ltd
Castle Place, 166 High Street, Lewes,
East Sussex BN7 1XU

Text © Alan Goodsell and Randall Maxey, 2018
Copyright in the Work © GMC Publications Ltd, 2018
ISBN 978 1 78494 408 7

Publisher Jonathan Bailey
Production Jim Bulley and Jo Pallett
Senior Project Editor Virginia Brehaut
Editor Sarah Doughty
Managing Art Editor Gilda Pacitti
Art Editor Rebecca Mothersole

Colour origination by GMC Reprographics
Printed and bound in China

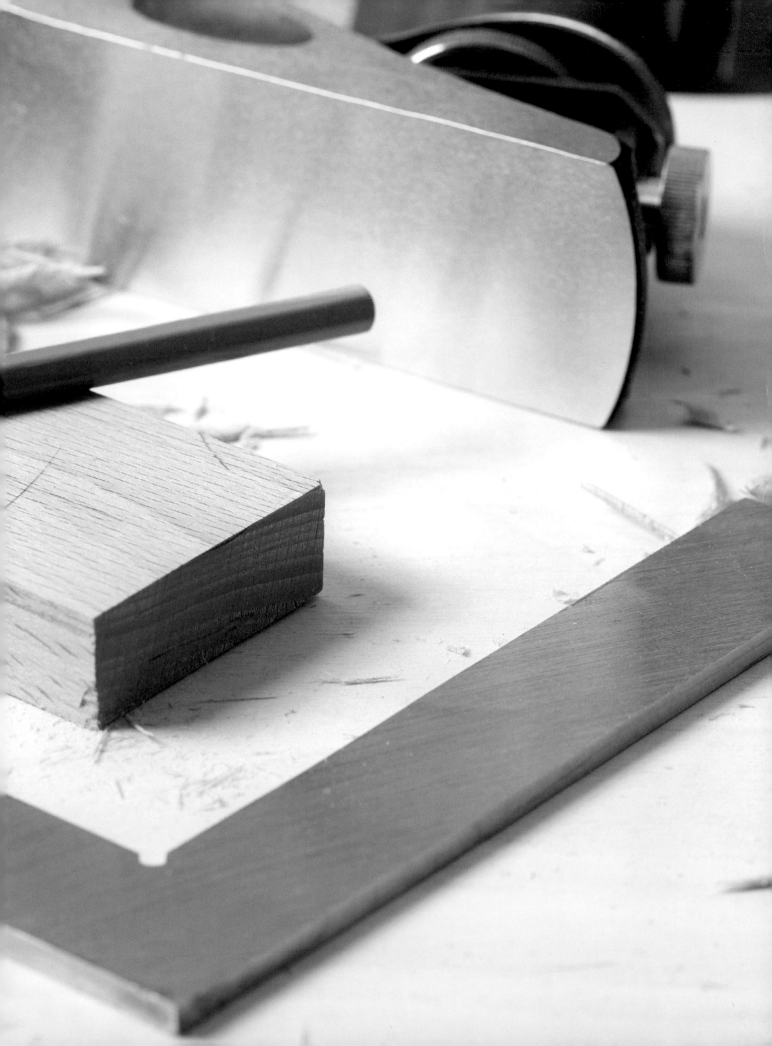

CONTENTS

INTRODUCTION

Woodworking is a very satisfying pastime. However, the skills needed to get good results will come easily to some, while others may find things more challenging. One of the reasons for finding woodworking difficult is trying to achieve tasks that are more complex than needed, then giving up in exasperation when they prove to be too hard. The secret is to take baby steps and learn things right from the start, then build your skills so that you can enjoy woodworking to the fullest. You can then spend your time making items that you can enjoy.

In this book we show you many aspects of woodworking, starting from the essential tools you need and tips on how to use them – all the way to how to create a series of approachable, but at the same time challenging, woodworking joints. After that you will move on to a selection of projects that you can make using the joints and techniques described. The items we show you how to make can be created exactly as shown if they suit your needs, but also can be easily modified by changing the dimensions to suit your own purposes.

The tools used are all non-power tools as they are inexpensive and readily available. This makes your introduction to woodworking much simpler and easier on the pocket. Using hand tools will also give you a much better insight into how this marvellous material that you are going to work with reacts to cutting and shaping – as the 'feel' for the wood can be lost when using power tools. The immersive use of hand tools will help you to understand, for example, what effect wood grain may have on a saw cut's direction, or whether the grain cut will close up and jam the saw.

You will need to practise and inevitably you will make mistakes, but that is how you learn. Making simple mistakes at this stage is not a problem because you are using inexpensive tools and materials. By the time you have covered all the basics in this book you will be able to call yourself a woodworker and continue to hone your skills with an enjoyable and satisfying pastime that will last a lifetime.

Happy and safe woodworking.

Alan Goodsell

WHAT IS WOOD?

Before beginning to work with wood it is important to understand this wonderful material. This section will give you an insight into the make-up and qualities of wood – this knowledge will help you to work it and appreciate it.

Many people think wood is an inert material like plastic or metal, but it couldn't be more different in its structure or handling. Wood comes from a living tree and, like all plants, trees depend on water for their existence. Water is gathered by the tree's roots and is then transported up through the tree, via root hairs, by a process called osmosis. Osmosis is the flow of one constituent of a solution through a semi-permeable membrane, while other constituents are unable to pass through it. The water carries other chemicals in it and is called sap. The sap then flows under pressure through the sapwood, or xylem, to the tree's crown.

New wood is produced by the cambium cell layer situated between the xylem and the phloem and completely encloses the living parts of the tree. During times of growth the cambial cells divide to produce new wood cells. The new wood is created on the existing core of wood and if this growth is seasonal the familiar annual growth rings of trees will form. As the tree grows, the inner layers of sapwood cease to function and the cells undergo a change to become heartwood. The new substances produced by this change give the heartwood its colour and characteristics.

Sawing and seasoning

Before trees become wood, there are some processes that have to be carried out. The first is to cut down the tree and then slice it into manageable pieces, which will be convenient sizes for use. Once the wood is sawn to size it needs to be dried out. Remember we mentioned earlier that trees are created with water and a freshly cut-down tree still retains a lot of water. Wood at this stage is called green wood.

If the wood is used when wet it will shrink as it dries out, making the things you create pretty much useless because they will distort. This means the wood needs to be dried out before use in a process called seasoning, which greatly reduces the wood's moisture content.

Cross-section through a tree, showing the layers of growth

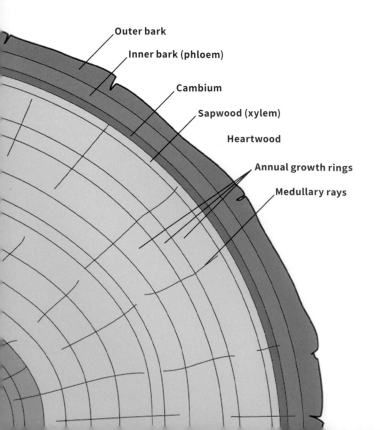

Outer bark

Inner bark (phloem)

Cambium

Sapwood (xylem)

Heartwood

Annual growth rings

Medullary rays

A slice through this tree clearly shows the annual growth rings.

Types of conversion

Heart is 'boxed' (cut square) and discarded

These boards are backsawn

Through-and-through sawing

Flat or plain sawing

Sawing

The tree can be sawn or 'converted' in different ways to make the best use of the wood. This can both reduce waste and obtain the best pieces for a specific purpose.

Through-and-through sawing is when a tree is sliced from end to end, in line with the grain. Wastage is minimal, but the boards may be prone to warping.

Flat or plain sawing is mostly the same as through-and-through, except that the middle section is sawn at a tangent to the grain to avoid including the unstable heart of the tree in the resulting boards. The centre section can be used for posts.

Traditional quartersawing is where the tree is sawn with the cuts radiating from the heart of the tree. This results in very stable boards but it does mean there is a lot of waste. This also makes the resulting boards very expensive.

Modern quartersawing is a mixture of plain sawing and traditional quartersawing, which reduces wastage and leaves wood in the centre than can be used as a 'post'.

Traditional quartersawing

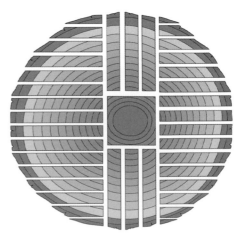

Modern quartersawing

The look of wood

The appearance of the grain in the finished wood surface depends on how that surface was oriented in the tree before conversion. The differences can be seen in three main ways: if the wood was cut at right angles to the annual rings, if the wood was cut at a tangent to the annual rings and if the boards were produced by sawing across the fibres. When you are in a timber yard you will be able to see these differences and pick the look you want. Be aware, though, that the prime cuts will be a lot more expensive than the lesser ones.

Seasoning

For woodworking purposes, wood is best used when it is dry. Dry wood is less likely to distort through the inevitable drying out that takes place in our indoor environments. When it is dry, wood is stronger.

Seasoning or drying wood will vary depending on what the wood is, how large the boards are and what they are intended for. There are two types of drying environments. One is in a kiln, the other is the air-dry method (out in the open air). The artificial environment of the kiln enables its dehumidifiers to work fast in drying out the wood. This can result in wood splitting, but can get the wood to a very dry condition quickly. The air-dry method is a lot slower but some people argue that the wood stabilizes better. However, the moisture content cannot be taken as low as in a kiln because of the ambient air moisture content.

Radial, tangential and transverse surfaces

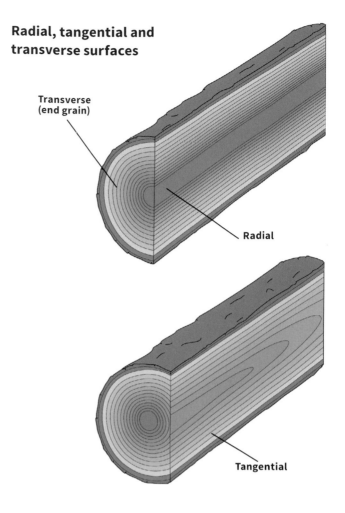

Transverse (end grain)

Radial

Tangential

A common technique in both methods is to stack the boards of wood and space them apart with small wood stickers. This allows air to pass between the boards and speed up the drying process. In the kiln the dehumidifiers move the air and air-drying relies on nature's breeze.

Boards of wood stacked for air-drying

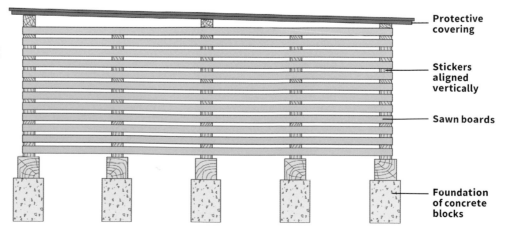

Protective covering

Stickers aligned vertically

Sawn boards

Foundation of concrete blocks

SAFETY

Woodworking is an inherently dangerous hobby and following the correct safety procedures and wearing good safety gear will help to protect you. Before using any new tool, always read the instructions and follow the recommended safety advice.

Lung and respiratory protection

Protecting your lungs is very important and fine particles of dust are a real health hazard to your breathing that is easily prevented. You will find dust masks come with various specifications to filter out different-sized particles. For woodworking look for the European P1–P3 basic masks (or a rating of N95 in the USA) and that will cover you for protection from wood dust and fumes. They are inexpensive and available from DIY stores. You could also consider the more expensive respirator-type masks. Remember that the mask will only work if you are wearing it so make putting one on part of your routine when woodworking.

Eye protection

Looking after your eyes is also important and particles of dust, particularly if they are flying off a power tool, can do untold damage to your eyes. Even just a cloud of dust will dry out your eyes, so you will need to wear eye protection in the form of glasses or goggles. These are easy to wear and ideal to combine with a dust mask. You might prefer to invest in a full-face vizor that covers your whole face, but they can be cumbersome and steam up when used with a dust mask.

Hearing protection

Protecting your hearing becomes apparent when you are using power tools as the action of machine-cutting wood creates a lot of noise. The simple way to combat this noise is to get some ear defenders or earplugs. They are readily available in DIY stores, so there is no excuse to not wear them – but they need to be easy to put on. If safety equipment is easy to use, this makes it more likely to be worn regularly.

Gloves

Some people like to wear gloves when working wood. Gloves can give a better grip on the tools you are using as well as holding the wood itself. You will also be protected from splinters and may also avoid blisters if you are hand sanding, for example.

SAFE WORKING PRACTICES

Apart from wearing safety equipment, you can also prevent yourself from harm by adopting safe working practices.

The first thing to do is to remove all jewellery. Necklaces, for example, can get trapped in tools and if rings get caught, they can cause a great deal of damage to your fingers.

Keeping your work area tidy is another good safety practice. Any piece of wood or tool left lying around on your bench can get in the way of your work. This may cause you to stop what you are doing, ruin a cut, or worst of all, you may find yourself caught up in a tool. Keep your work area clear of dust and debris for a safer work experience.

A tidy bench, tied-back hair and all jewellery removed makes for a safe workplace.

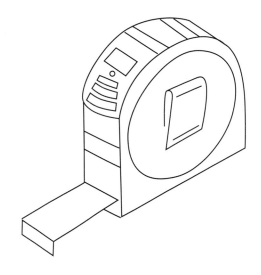

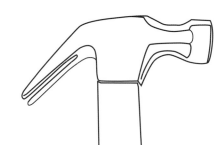

BASIC TOOLS

In any hobby or craft, the tools you need to get for it can be extensive and become expensive. In woodworking, this is also the case, but with just the few basic tools shown here, you will be able to achieve a huge amount of satisfying work. This chapter is a guide to what tools you might want to get. How you use the tools is covered later in the book.

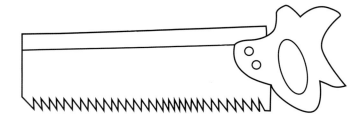

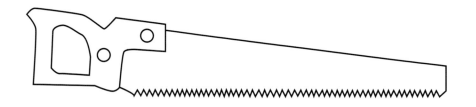

HAMMERS

The hammer is thought to be the most basic woodworking tool and is simply a heavy weight on a stick to strike nails and drive them into a piece of wood. However, there is much more to a hammer than this and there are variations of hammer that are made for specific tasks.

Claw hammer

The most common hammer used for woodworking is the claw hammer. This has a broad hammer head and on the reverse side of it is a curved, split device, which is used for removing nails.

Ball-peen hammer

Another hammer that you may see is the ball-peen hammer. This hammer is used for metalworking. The ball is used to pound metal and shape it. You can use this hammer in the workshop but its uses are limited.

Cross-peen hammer

The cross-peen hammer is a small hammer specifically designed for nailing small nails called pins or brads into wood.

HAZARD WARNING

The term 'peen' for hammers is the process, called peening, used for hardening the metal surface of a hammer. This is achieved by either pounding, shot blasting or using a laser light to alter the surface of the hammer head's metal. An important thing to remember is that this hardening process makes the hammer head brittle, so NEVER hit two hammer heads together as shards of metal will shatter off and become shrapnel, an extremely dangerous hazard.

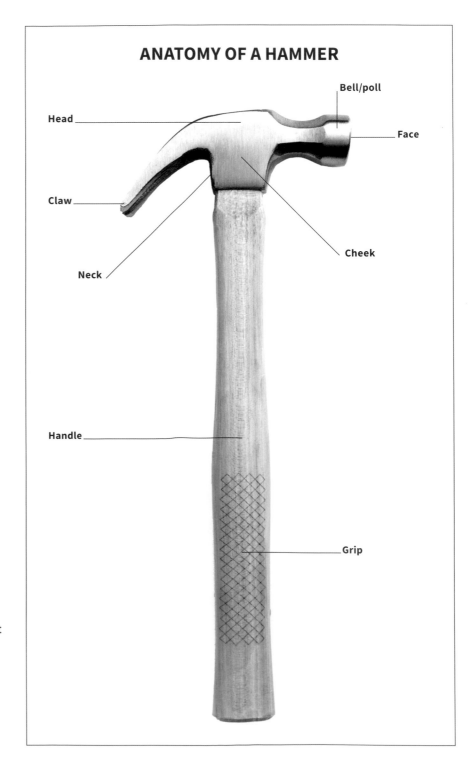

ANATOMY OF A HAMMER

Bell/poll

Head

Face

Claw

Cheek

Neck

Handle

Grip

The claw hammer **1** is the most common hammer seen in the workshop. **2** The ball-peen hammer can be used in the workshop but is a rather cumbersome metalworking tool. The cross-peen hammer **3** is used for nailing in small nails called pins or brads. **4** A wooden-handled hammer is versatile and gives good feedback. **5** The same hammer in an all-metal construction is strong and will last a lifetime.

Handles and sizes

The handles of hammers are either made of wood or metal. Wooden-handled hammers tend to give better feedback to the hand as there is a little flexibility and it is also possible to change the handle if it becomes damaged. Metal-handled hammers are better for brute force and the head and handle are forged in one piece to make them immensely strong. All the hammers mentioned here come in various sizes that will be specific to the type of work they will be used for, or even just the user's personal preference.

Mallets

The mallet is also in the hammer family and is used generally for striking wood. The head is made of wood, or even dense rubber, and is designed to not damage what is being hit. Mallets can be used for 'persuading' pieces of wood with a joint to fit together, and a popular use is to tap the end of a chisel to give a controlled cut. Mallet heads are generally an angled rectangular shape when used for persuading. Turned, round heads are used on mallets used for chiselling, and a popular wood for this is the green-hued lignum vitae (*Guaiacum officinale*) – a wood so dense it does not float in water. There are other mallet head shapes available and their roles can be interchanged, depending on your preferences.

6 A turned wooden-head mallet is the best choice for tapping chisels. A traditional rectangular wooden mallet **7** is a good general-purpose tool. A dense rubber mallet **8** is a useful tool to have for adjusting things.

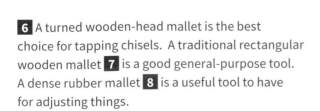

HANDSAWS

Choosing the right handsaw for the job can be confusing as there are so many types of saw. We will guide you here to select the saw that will work for you. The saw you need probably isn't necessarily the most expensive one you can buy.

The saw cuts wood using its teeth and the forward and backward motion supplied by the operator's arm. The teeth of the saw can be small and close together (fine toothed) or large and far apart (coarse toothed) and anywhere in between. This spacing is called the TPI or teeth per inch.

The teeth also have what is called a 'set' and this is where the teeth are slightly bent sideways and every alternate tooth is bent in the opposite direction. When the saw's teeth pass through the wood, they cut a slot slightly wider than the thickness of the saw's blade and stop it binding or getting trapped in the slot. This slot is called the 'kerf' and is essential for ensuring the saw blade cuts properly. The hook of the tooth creates a little chisel on the end of the tooth and this is what cuts the wood. It is also what drags the sawdust out of the slot to make sure it doesn't build up.

In Western countries, the teeth of a saw point forwards meaning the saw cuts on the push stroke. However, in some Eastern countries, such as Japan, for example, saws have their teeth pointing backwards, meaning the saw cuts on the pull stroke. Both types of saw cut well, but the Japanese saws can be made of thinner steel and therefore produce a thinner kerf. For accurate cutting across the wood's grain a fine-tooth saw is the one to use, and for a rip cut along the wood's grain a coarse-tooth saw is best (see page 44).

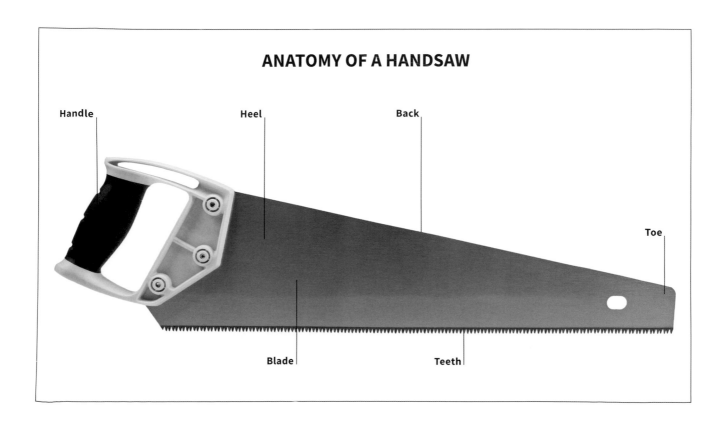

ANATOMY OF A HANDSAW

Handle   Heel   Back   Toe

Blade   Teeth

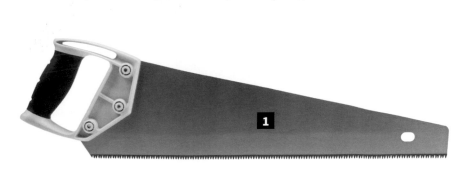

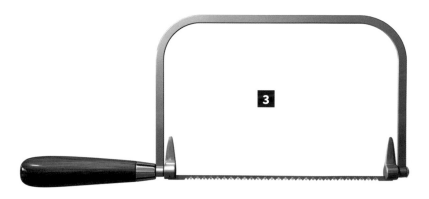

If you only buy one saw, the panel saw **1** is probably the one you will make the most use of. The tenon saw **2** is a specialized saw for cutting complex joints. The coping saw **3** is a surprisingly versatile tool – you won't regret buying one.

Panel saw

A panel saw is the most widely used saw and can be your general-purpose saw of choice. These saws are available in a wide range of sizes and tooth coarseness. The high-end saws that furniture makers use have blades that are made from high carbon steel; this type of steel is flexible and can be sharpened to a high degree. The downside is that the sharp edge does not last long and the blade will often need sharpening. Modern saws that are available from a DIY store are made using a composite steel and the teeth are hardened to make their sharpness last a long time. They may not be quite as sharp as the furniture maker's saw, but for most purposes you are unlikely to notice the difference. You will find that they are cheap, readily available and no knowledge of sharpening is required.

Tenon saw

The tenon saw is a highly specialized saw that is typically used to cut complex joints such as dovetail joints. The reinforced spine ensures that the blade is kept straight but will not allow a cut to be made past it. It is a useful saw to have and it is used in the making of the projects in this book.

Coping saw

This is a saw you will probably want in your tool collection. It has a fine, thin blade that is held in a U-shaped metal frame with a handle that twists to tighten the blade. This saw allows shaped cuts to be made and can be used for cutting complex shapes in the back splat of chairs, scribing mouldings together to create a 'coped' joint. This is where the saw gets its name, and describes the method of cutting the profile of a moulding into the end of another piece, so that when they are placed together at right angles it looks like a tight joint.

Fret saw

The fret saw is like a coping saw, but has a much larger frame and finer blade. While useful to know about it, this isn't a saw that you are likely to need at the moment. It is normally used for cutting complex shapes, such as the pieces for a jigsaw puzzle, for example.

Pad saw

The pad saw goes by several different names including keyhole saw, compass saw, jab saw, alligator saw and more. The saw is basically a handle that the narrow blade can be held in and positioned with only part of the blade out of the handle. This is to help prevent the blade from flexing, as only the amount of blade you need is exposed. The purpose of this saw is to be able to make curved cuts, using only a hole in the wood to get started. This isn't a saw that you will use every day but it is always useful to have one just in case. As with all saws, they come in different sizes and blade material variations.

A fret saw **4** is used to cut complex shapes. A pad saw **5** is used for cutting difficult shapes, such as the holes for door locks and where space is restricted.

tips and tricks
STOP WOOD SPLINTERING

When sawing all the way through a piece of wood, make sure the section that will be released by the saw cut is well supported. This will ensure that the weight of the wood does not drag it down and break the remaining part of the cut, causing the wood fibres to splinter.

SCREWDRIVERS

After nails, screws are the best way to hold pieces of wood together. Screws will hold tightly and a small collection of screwdrivers will be invaluable for assembling projects as well as attaching hardware.

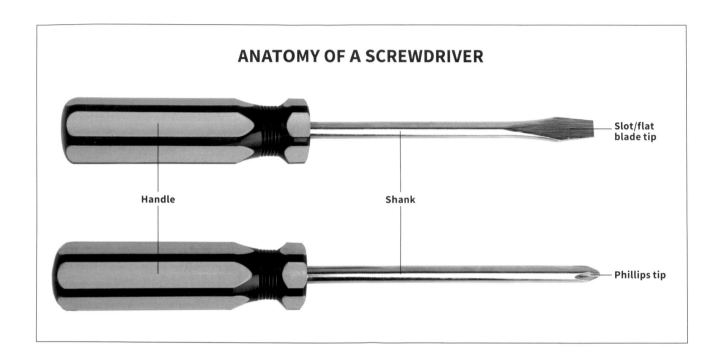

ANATOMY OF A SCREWDRIVER

Handle

Shank

Slot/flat blade tip

Phillips tip

Types of screwdriver

There are many types of screwdriver and it is important to make sure the tip matches the head of the screw being used. The main kinds of screwdriver tips used in woodworking are the slot/flat tip and the Phillips tip. For the slot/flat type, make sure that the thickness of the tip is close to the same size of the head of the screw; it should be no wider that the diameter of the head. The Phillips tip is a crosshead-type, but there are other versions that look similar. Although it is possible to mix them, you will damage a screwdriver by doing so.

Handle design

Screwdriver handles are used to give you the best grip for the job in hand. The old and trusted bulbous shape of the cabinetmaker's handle (originally in wood) is our personal preference for good grip. Nowadays most screwdrivers have plastic handles. While the bulbous handle is still available, there is also the fluted-type handle that can give a good twisting grip. There are plenty of 'ergonomic' shaped handles and you will want to try some out to see which ones you prefer.

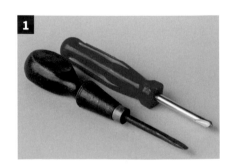

1 The wooden cabinetmaker's handle, on the left, is our preferred shape for a good grip. On the right is a modern plastic fluted-handle design.

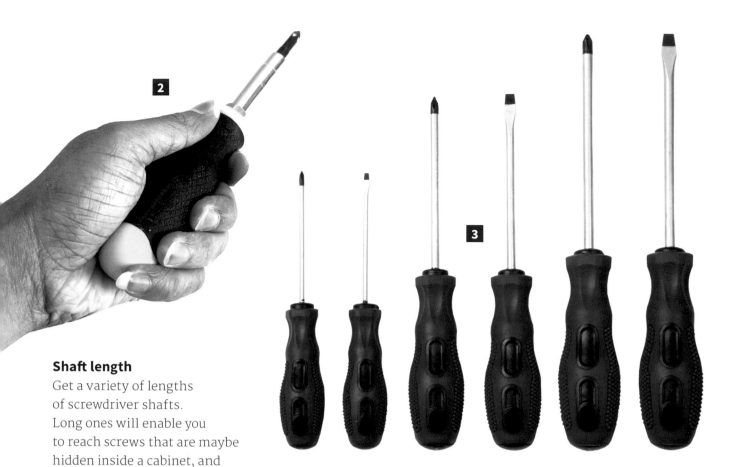

Shaft length

Get a variety of lengths of screwdriver shafts. Long ones will enable you to reach screws that are maybe hidden inside a cabinet, and short ones give you good control where screws are easily accessible. A mid-length screwdriver is a useful one to have for general purposes.

Construction type

Lastly, there are different types of screwdriver construction. The one-piece type where the shaft has the driver tip forged into the end of it is a very strong option. The other type is the interchangeable tip version. These are useful to have as you only need a selection of tips to complete your screwdriver set. If you find that you need a tip you don't have, it is a simple matter of getting a new tip and not a whole new screwdriver. There is often storage in the handle for spare tips.

An 'ergonomic' design handle **2** is also a sensible choice for a good grip. Get a set of screwdrivers in different lengths **3** to make sure you cover all options. A good option for versatility is the interchangeable tip screwdriver **4**. It is inexpensive to own a screwdriver tip **5** for every screw type available.

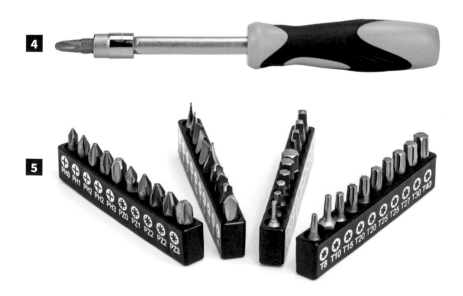

CHISELS

The chisel is an important tool in woodworking and mastering cutting with one is relatively easy. Chisels are used for cutting joints and for paring slivers of wood to trim them to length or make a joint fit.

You will be best advised to get a set of general-purpose chisels to start with. Like most other woodworking tools, the modern versions of chisels come with plastic handles and there will be a variety of lengths to choose from. Remember that a sharp chisel will cut you just as easily as it will cut the wood, so make sure you read the using hand tools section (see pages 52–55).

The two types of chisel that are worth your consideration for basic woodworking are the plain-edge and the bevel-edge chisel (see opposite). If you are browsing a woodworking website or online store you will probably see a wide range of other types of chisel too. These will be most likely used for woodturning or woodcarving and we won't be covering them in this book as they need a whole different set of skills to use them.

ANATOMY OF A CHISEL

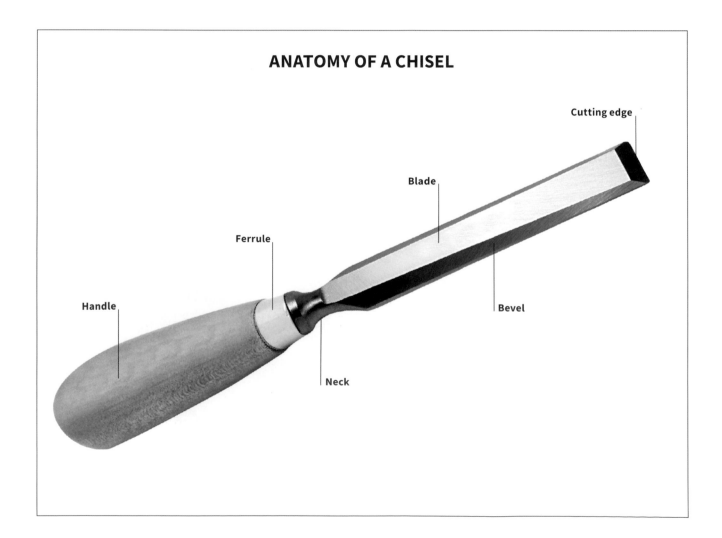

Cutting edge

Blade

Bevel

Ferrule

Handle

Neck

Plain-edge chisels

This is the standard chisel and can be used for all general-purpose chiselling. The shape of the metal chisels are made from has square edges, which gives the chisels the maximum rigidity if you happen to be levering out waste wood with them. They are the least expensive chisels to buy as they are the easiest to make. A small set of these chisels will give you the different widths you are likely to need and you will use them often.

Bevel-edge chisels

Bevel-edge chisels look almost identical to the plain-edge chisel but you will see a bevel on the top edges of the chisel blade. This bevel is to allow the chisel to gain access into a tapered recess such as a dovetail joint. Although we will not cover complex joints here, these chisels are well worth an investment to complement your plain-edge set.

1 These plain-edge chisels are robust tools used for most chiselling work. **2** A bevel-edge chisel allows access into tapered recesses.

Sharpening stone

It is also useful to get a sharpening stone and guide as your chisels will get blunt quite quickly. Getting a sharp edge back on each chisel is not a difficult process (see page 55) and something you will be able to do yourself. In addition to the stone you will also need some cutting oil to protect the stone and carry away the debris. Do not use oil on a water stone.

Sharpening stones will keep a sharp edge on your chisel. The selection here shows coarse and fine grits. Some have different grits on each side.

DRILLS AND DRILL BITS

Drilling holes in wood is one of the staple techniques of woodworking. There is a variety of drilling tools and drill bits available and you will definitely want to consider one or all of these as a purchase.

Hand drill

The hand drill is a much-underestimated tool and we would urge you to always keep one handy in your toolbox. We live in a world of power tools and while they are thought to be the best way of doing things, this is not necessarily so. Drilling is one of those tasks that can easily be done by hand (see page 50). The hand drill is inexpensive, versatile and always ready to go as it doesn't need electrical power.

1 A hand drill is a useful and inexpensive addition to your toolkit. You might find a vintage one like this in a second-hand tool shop.

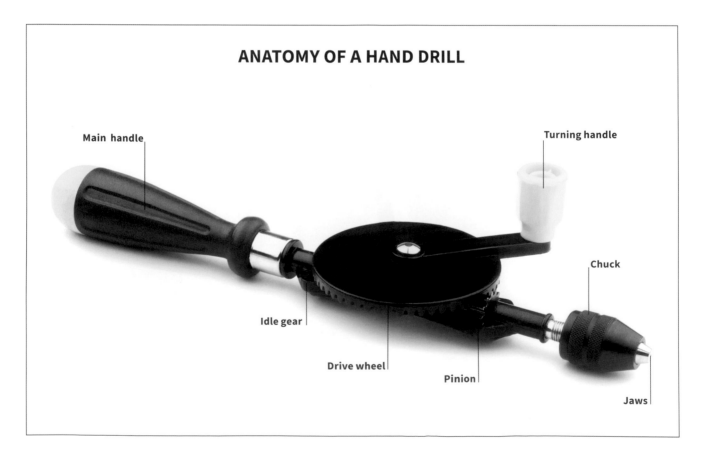

ANATOMY OF A HAND DRILL

Main handle

Turning handle

Chuck

Idle gear

Drive wheel

Pinion

Jaws

Drill bits

Drill bits come in different types too, and the one we are most familiar with is the regular twist bit – and a set of these will be in constant use. They can be used in metal or wood. Another type of twist drill bit is almost identical to the one previously mentioned, but has a little point on the tip. This is used for jabbing into the wood before drilling and ensures the hole will be in exactly the right place. This is called a wood bit.

For drilling larger holes, the bit to use is the flat or spade bit, and a set of these is also inexpensive and a useful addition to your toolkit. A much more expensive option for large-hole drilling is the Forstner bit. This is more like a rotary chisel that will produce an extremely accurate hole and is most likely to be used by furniture makers.

2 The twist bit is on the right, the flat/spade bit in the middle and the Forstner bit on the left.

3 This set of drill bits has regular twist bits – HSS (High Speed Steel) wood and metal bits – wood bits with a spur on the tip and for good measure a few masonry bits.

Cordless drills

Every woodworker will have, or want to get, a cordless drill. We would not be without one and no doubt you will want to get one too. See page 35 for more details on power tools.

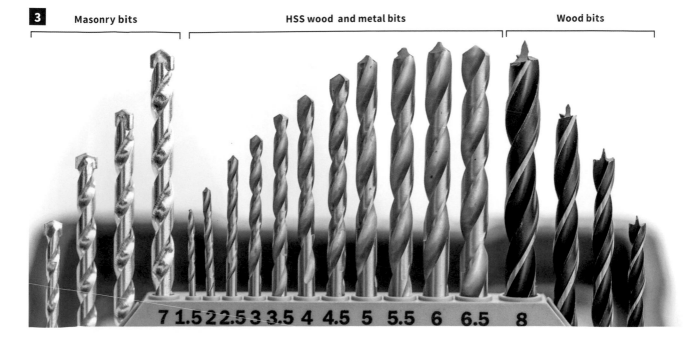

3 Masonry bits | HSS wood and metal bits | Wood bits

7 1.5 2 2.5 3 3.5 4 4.5 5 5.5 6 6.5 8

HAND PLANES

The hand plane is a wood-smoothing tool that is easy to hold to remove a shaving of wood and leaves an extremely smooth surface.

The hand plane works by having a wide, thin chisel-like blade held at a specific angle in its frame. The blade has a sharp edge that protrudes slightly below the 'sole' or underside of the plane. When the plane is pushed along the surface of a piece of wood the blade removes a wide sliver of wood from it, making it smooth. You may well ask 'why not just use sandpaper?' to do this task

– and the answer is that the plane will remove more wood than sandpaper and leave a much smoother flat surface. There is a bit of a learning curve to master smooth hand planing (see page 56), but it is time well spent to get the best results. Once mastered, it is an amazing hand tool and one that skilled woodworkers will have a wide selection of.

ANATOMY OF A HAND PLANE

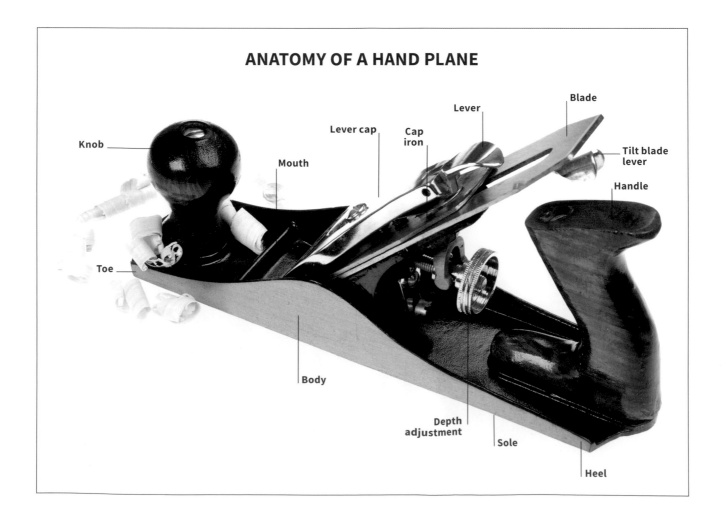

Knob · Mouth · Lever cap · Cap iron · Lever · Blade · Tilt blade lever · Handle · Toe · Body · Depth adjustment · Sole · Heel

Types of hand plane

There are two types of plane that we would recommend for the beginner woodworker and they are the smoothing plane and the block plane.

The smoothing plane is the larger of the two planes and it does exactly what is it says it does: it is used to smooth the surface of wood. The block plane is easily held in one hand and this is the tool we use to remove small bumps from wood. It can also be used at an angle on the edge of a piece of wood to remove the sharp corner (see page 57), or to use the correct term, 'arris', quickly and easily.

1 A block plane is great tool to quickly 'knock off' the sharp corners of a piece of wood. **2** A smoothing plane takes some practice to master, but is well worth the effort.

MEASURING AND MARKING

Most people have heard the saying 'measure twice, cut once' – an essential piece of information to remember when woodworking. Not only is cutting a piece of wood the wrong size frustrating and time consuming, but it is also wasteful and expensive.

Steel rule

The most useful measuring tool for your workshop will be the steel rule and it is more versatile that you might first imagine. Steel rules are more useful than the plastic variants as they are more durable and the measurements are easier to see. The USA uses the imperial (or English, as they call it) measuring system (with inches divided into fractions of an inch) and most of the rest of the world uses the metric system as centimetres (divided into millimetres). It is worth getting a rule that has both metric and imperial measurements on it as you will no doubt encounter both types of system when you work on projects.

Tape measure

For measuring longer items, a tape measure is the tool to have. Like the steel rule, it is worth getting one that has both measuring systems on the tape. It is also worth investing in a more expensive and better quality one to ensure it will last longer.

Adjustable or sliding bevel

A tool for measuring angles is the adjustable bevel, or sliding bevel. The rule not only slides through the main body, but can also be locked at an angle. This is useful if you want to mark an angle on a piece of wood that matches the angle on something else.

Combination square

Marking tools for woodworking are many and varied, but we have selected a couple of tools that you may want to get. Again, these come in many variations, including the traditional woodworking square. This a great tool to have as it is accurate and simple to use. However, an even better option is the combination square. This is a versatile tool that will allow you to mark lines at both right angles and 45°. The rule part of the tool can be slid through the body so can be used for measuring too. Some of these tools have a bubble level built-in, which can be a useful feature, but probably not one that you will use much at this stage.

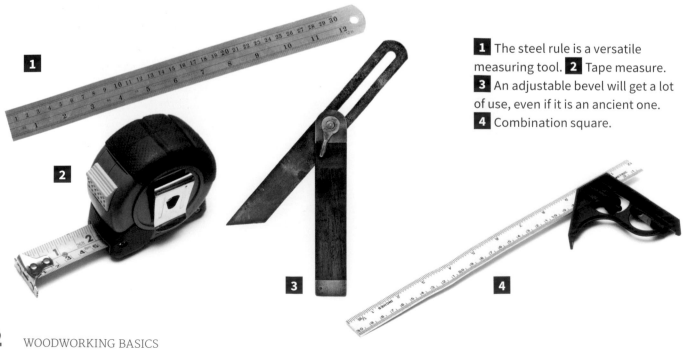

1 The steel rule is a versatile measuring tool. **2** Tape measure. **3** An adjustable bevel will get a lot of use, even if it is an ancient one. **4** Combination square.

ANATOMY OF A COMBINATION SQUARE

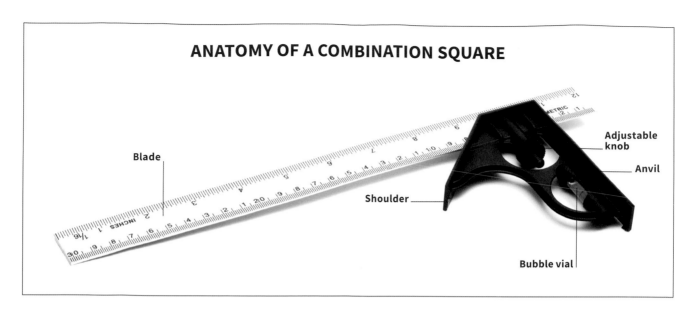

Blade

Adjustable knob

Anvil

Shoulder

Bubble vial

ANATOMY OF A TAPE MEASURE

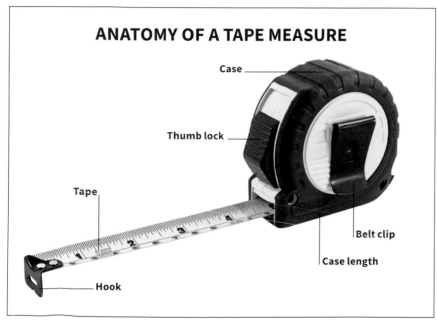

Case

Thumb lock

Tape

Belt clip

Case length

Hook

The pencil

A pencil is the best tool for the job when making marks for sawing. Some people like to use the flat carpenter's pencil, but we are happy to use a regular pencil. Use a pencil with a medium hardness lead such as an HB, as this will mark the surface well and keep sharp for a decent number of marks before needing to be sharpened again.

Box-cutter

Another marking tool is a knife and a simple box-cutter is all you need. Cutting a line in the surface of a piece of wood is a common technique in woodworking as it will cut the wood fibres, ensuring a clean edge to a saw cut. Not only can you use your knife for cutting a mark in the surface of your wood, but you can also use it to sharpen your pencil.

5 Most marking on wood is best done with a pencil. Either a flat carpenter's pencil or a regular pencil will do the job. **6** A simple box-cutter makes a good marking tool. It is easy to keep sharp by snapping off the blade to reveal a new sharp edge.

5

6

CLAMPS

Holding pieces of wood together or holding them to a bench while working on them is the job of the clamp. This is a device that has two jaws that can be tightened together, holding whatever is in between them.

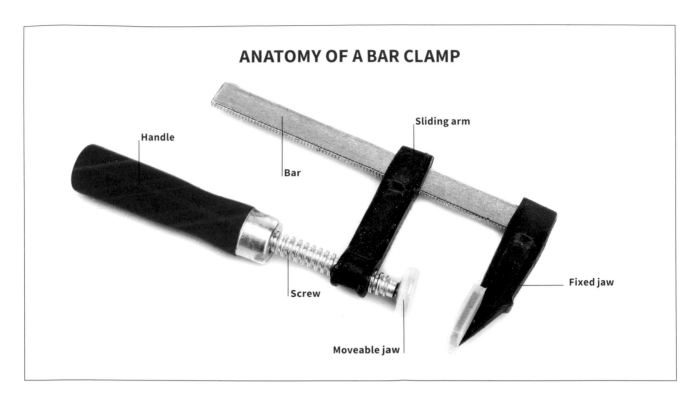

ANATOMY OF A BAR CLAMP

Handle

Sliding arm

Bar

Screw

Moveable jaw

Fixed jaw

Bar clamp

There are many types of clamp, but the one that will do most jobs is the bar clamp (pictured above). Bar clamps have a pair of jaws that close together, holding pieces together between them. They are inexpensive and easily available so you can afford to get hold of a few of them. Getting different-sized ones is also a good idea as they will suit many different types of work.

1 Here the pieces of wood are being glued together. The clamps hold them in place until it is dry.

POWER TOOLS

There are specialized power tools available for every aspect of woodworking, but these are something that you will work your way towards as your woodworking skills progress.

For general woodworking tasks, there are a few power tools that might help you out and the few mentioned here are the least expensive power tools and most useful ones you might want. However, before buying any of them, consider if they will help you in your early days of woodworking and if not, postpone getting them until later.

Power drill

A power drill, cordless or mains power, can be useful for drilling holes instead of using the hand drill, but for putting in screws we think they are overused and can be too powerful. Screwing by hand (see page 46) will educate you in how wood reacts to being penetrated by screws, and also to learn the correct way to screw pieces of wood together.

Pillar drill

A benchtop power tool worth mentioning is the pillar drill or drill press. This is a much more specialized tool that will give a precision that hand-held drills can't match, especially if you want to drill a hole at precise right angles to the surface of your wood. A small benchtop one won't break the bank or take up much space in your workshop. This would be worth considering at a later time, when your woodworking skills increase.

1 The mid-sized power drill makes light work of drilling holes, but is probably too powerful for screwing in screws.

2 A benchtop pillar drill, or drill press, need not be an expensive investment and will be worth it later when your woodworking skills increase.

Nail gun

Everyone who watches a home DIY show will often see a small nail gun being used for connecting pieces of wood together. This might seem like a good and fast way of doing the job, but in our opinion it is just lazy and like using a sledgehammer to crack a walnut.

Power saw

Power saws are tools best left until your woodworking confidence grows. The jigsaw, circular saw and mitre saw can make light work of cutting wood. However, they are powerful and potentially dangerous and should be used after some training, preferably by attending a class.

Router

Another specialized woodworking power tool is the router. This is widely acknowledged as the most versatile woodworking power tool but you will definitely want to learn how to use one under supervision. The things you can do with a router are virtually endless, but the gyroscopic force, the weird effect caused by the router's motor spinning, can be scary and will put a lot of people off using one.

Sander

The last power tool we will mention is the sander. There are different ones available and they will make light work of smoothing wood. If you are going to get one, make sure the first one you get is a random-orbit sander, which leaves less swirly marks on the wood than a regular rotary sander.

Leave the nail gun to contractors, who need to fix things together fast.

Power saws can make light work of cutting wood. Like all power saws, the circular saw seen here should be used after training and with care.

The router is the most versatile power tool in the shop, but routers are expensive and it is a steep learning curve to understand how to use one safely.

A useful power sander to get is the random-orbit sander.

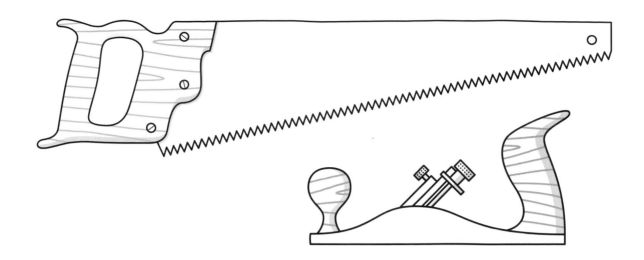

USING HAND TOOLS

Using woodworking tools well is a skill that is easily learned. In this chapter, you will learn the very basics of using the hand tools most commonly needed for woodworking, along with useful tips that will help you to use them more productively and safely.

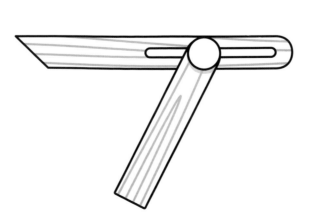

HOW TO USE A HAMMER

Using a hammer to drive in nails sounds easy but it is still a tool that you need to use correctly and safely, so you hit the nail squarely with a direct hit each time.

Holding a hammer

The first thing to get right when hammering is how to grip the hammer. The woodworking hammer is used with a little more finesse than a metalworking hammer so achieving a good hold on it is essential.

Imagine you are going to shake hands with someone, but hold the hammer's handle instead of a hand. Grip the handle close to the end as this will give you the most leverage and allow the hammer to work to its full potential. It is a common mistake to hold a hammer halfway along the handle and this will give poor results because of a lack of control and leverage. This is called 'choking' the hammer.

This is the grip to use on a hammer; note that the hand is placed towards the end of the handle and at the point of impact the face of the hammer's head is at right angles to the nail.

Hammering a nail

Put a nail between your finger and thumb of your non-hammering hand; hold it near the head so your fingers aren't trapped on the immovable wood – this can be painful if you miss the nail and hit your fingers by mistake. Set the point of the nail on the wood in the position you want to drive it in, then tap the head of the nail a couple of times to get it to penetrate the wood and stay in place. This will also help you to position yourself so that the face of the hammer's head is at right angles to the nail and the hammer to achieve a powerful strike; a bit like a test swing in golf. When hammering, keep your eye on the nail and not on the hammer and this will ensure you hit it every time.

Move the hand that was holding the nail away and repeatedly strike the nail with the head of the hammer to drive it in with each stroke, until it is all the way in. If you are using a small cross-peen hammer (see page 18), use your wrist for the swinging action and if using a larger claw hammer (see page 18) use your elbow to achieve the swinging action. You do not need to exert a lot of force as the weight of the hammer and a good swing will do most of the work.

When hammering, make sure that the hammer does not drive in the nail so far that its head bruises the surface of the wood, as this will look unsightly. When the nail is just proud of the wood's surface you can drive it below the surface of the wood by hammering onto a nail punch (see picture 6) positioned on the nail's head to keep the hammer away from doing damage. Wood filler can be used to fill the recess left by the sunken nail head.

Before hammering, hold the nail between the finger and thumb.

Preparing to hammer a small nail.

Small nails need a wrist action when swinging the hammer.

Preparing to hammer a large nail.

Large nails need an elbow action when swinging the hammer.

Use a nail punch to recess the nail's head, before filling it with wood filler.

Pins and brads

You can turn the hammer around and hold the flat peen (the opposite side of the hammer's head) between your nail-holding fingers to hammer in small nails, pins or brads. If you don't have a flat peen, you can push a nail, pin or brad though a piece of thin card and then hold the card to keep your fingers out of the way using the face of the hammer. The card is easily removed once the nail is inserted into the wood.

The flat peen is used to strike small nails, pins or brads.

Use a piece of card to hold a pin or brad to keep your fingers out of the hammer's way.

Removing nails

The claw on a claw hammer is used for removing nails. The taper of the claw is slid under the head of the nail and the curved surface of the claw is used, in conjunction with the hammer's handle, to lever the nail out of the wood. It is a good idea to place a pad under the claw to prevent it damaging the wood. To gain more leverage as the nail comes out of the wood, you can place blocks under the claw.

Place a pad and block underneath the claw when using it to remove nails.

tips and tricks
SPLITTING WOOD

A common problem when nailing close to the end of a piece of wood is that the wood splits because the nail's point is tapered, and this spreads the fibres of the wood, causing them to split apart. Turning the nail over on a metal surface and simply tapping the point of the nail to make it blunt can prevent this.

A nail with a blunt point will tear the fibres of the wood as it is hammered in, effectively cutting a hole for it to go through and thus eliminating a split. Alternatively, a more time-consuming way to achieve this is to drill a pilot hole in the wood and lubricate the nail with wax or soap.

Blunt the end of a nail to stop the wood splitting.

HOW TO USE A SAW

Sawing wood is an essential skill to be mastered. But before you even start, you need to determine which sort of saw you need for the job, which depends on what you will be cutting.

Choosing a saw

Selecting which saw to use depends on whether you are cutting with or against the wood grain. For ripping (along the grain of the wood) use a coarse-tooth saw and for cutting across the grain use a fine-tooth saw. For general use, a panel-type saw (see page 22) will be the best option and you can progress to more specialist saws later. All the panel saws used here have hardened teeth so no sharpening is required.

Sawing a piece of wood

Mark where on the wood you want to cut (see page 63). Follow this mark to guide your saw in the correct place. Remember always to measure twice and cut once. You can't undo a saw cut, so if it is wrong you have wasted a piece of wood.

Place the teeth of the saw that are near to the end of the saw (away from the handle) on the waste side of the marked line. Use your thumb on the side of the saw blade, well clear of the teeth to give it support. Push the saw sharply forwards and this will start the cut. This is a lot easier when making a rip cut along the grain than across the grain. The saw cut has now started.

Continue to push the saw back and forth with the forward stroke being the cutting stroke. Once the saw cut, or kerf, is deep enough to hold the saw in place, move your thumb away from the blade. Don't apply any pressure to the saw as the teeth will do all the cutting; just make sure that you are positioned in such a way to be able to smoothly move your arm back and forth, ensuring that you have unobstructed movement to help keep the cut straight and true. Use a stroke that uses most of the length of the saw blade to make the cut. If you have aligned yourself properly the saw will cut along the line you have marked. It takes some practice to make sure the saw is upright to make the vertical cut.

Keeping a straight and smooth line

No matter how skilled you are at sawing, there is a tendency for the cut to veer offline. This can be counteracted by very slightly changing the angle that the saw is in relation to the cut in the wood. In this way, it is possible to steer the saw along a line; again, this is a skill that is mastered with practice.

Applying wax to the saw blade can make it run smoother in the kerf. A candle rubbed lightly on either side of the blade is all that is needed to reduce friction.

Saws come with different teeth types. Fine-tooth ones are generally used for crosscutting and coarse-tooth ones for ripsawing along the grain.

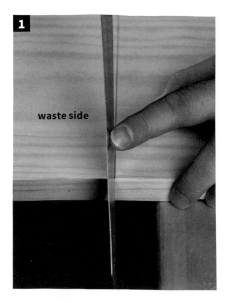

Place the saw on the waste side of the mark and use a finger or thumb to guide the saw's blade.

Push the saw forward sharply to start the cut.

A good grip on the saw's handle will help control the direction of the cut. Use a smooth forwards and backwards action, with the full length of the blade, and the saw will do all the work.

tips and tricks
SAWING ALONG AND ACROSS THE GRAIN

When cutting along the grain there is a possibility that the saw cut will release tension in the wood and close the kerf and pinch the saw blade. If this happens, place a thin wedge in the kerf to keep it open so it doesn't trap the saw blade. For sawing across the grain, the best angle for the saw is 45° and for ripping along the grain, a good angle for the saw is 60°.

Saw at 45° when sawing across the grain.

Saw at 60° when rip-cutting with the grain.

HOW TO USE A SCREWDRIVER

Driving screws into wood by hand with a screwdriver is quite a satisfying thing to do. You get a feel for the material you are working with and often the result is better than using a power tool because you can feel when the screw is tight and not overtighten it.

Head and tip types

It is important to match the screwdriver tip with the head type of the screw (see page 24). When using a slot-head screw, make sure that the thickness of the screwdriver's tip is close in size to the screw's slot. Also make sure that the screwdriver tip is not wider than the diameter of the screw head, as this will damage the wood.

When using a crosshead-type screw, make sure that the screwdriver tip fits tightly in the screw's head. Most commonly used is the Phillips head (see page 24), but there are a few variations of the crosshead-type screw that all look alike. However, if you try and use an incorrect tip you are likely to damage the screwdriver's tip, or the screw's head.

Holding a screwdriver

It is essential to hold a screwdriver correctly and your choice of handle will play a part in this. Find a handle type that is comfortable for you and will give you a good grip. Also ensure that the shaft of the screwdriver is in line with your arm so it can rotate when you twist your arm.

Driving in a screw

You will need to practise the first stage of screwing into wood to ensure good results. Place the point of the screw where you want it to be and place the screwdriver's tip in the screw's head. It can help if you use a finger and thumb to hold both the screw and screwdriver tip together. Push slightly to drive the point of the screw into the wood and then start turning the screwdriver clockwise. Very little pressure is required as the thread of the screw will engage in the wood and start pulling the screw in. Move your fingers away from the screw's head and use them to hold the shaft of the screwdriver to give it stability. Make sure the screwdriver is in line with the screw to ensure the screwdriver tip is correctly seated in the screw's head. Continue driving the screw into the wood until it is all the way home.

---

tips and tricks
ADDING LUBRICATION

When using a screwdriver to drive screws into hardwood or similar, it can help if some lubrication is applied to the thread of the screw. Wax or soap can be used, but make sure that none of this is left on the surface of the wood as it may impair the staining and finishing process.

Apply some wax or soap to the screw thread to lubricate it.

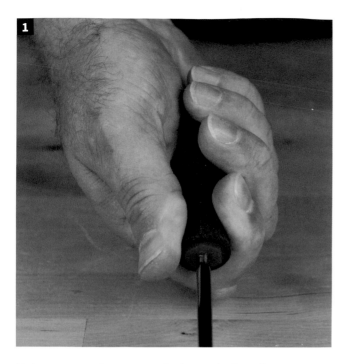

Make sure you have a good grip on the handle of the screwdriver.

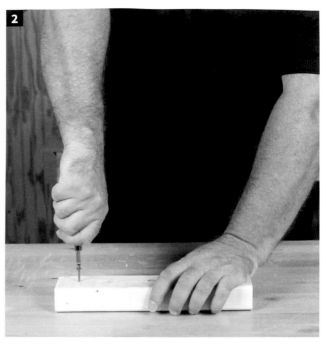

Line up your arm with the shaft of the screwdriver to ensure a smooth rotating action.

Hold the screw tip in the screw head to start.

Now move your fingers away and continue driving the screw into the wood.

Clearance and pilot holes

To make driving screws in easier there are some techniques that can be used. The clearance hole is one and the pilot hole is another. The clearance hole is drilled in the first piece of wood of two pieces you want to screw together. Establish where you want to place the screw and then drill a clearance hole in the first piece of wood. This hole needs to be the same size as the outside diameter of the screw so is doesn't bind or catch on the thread of the screw. Use a countersink to create a small recess for the screw's head, see photo 4.

The pilot hole is drilled in the second piece of wood and this hole is the size of the inner part of the screw's thread. This gives that part of the screw clearance, but ensures that the thread of the screw cuts into the wood to give it a good grip. This is done to ensure that when the screw is screwed in the two pieces of wood are pulled tightly together. A clearance and pilot hole will make sure there is no debris between the wood faces, ensure that your screw is straight and help prevent splitting.

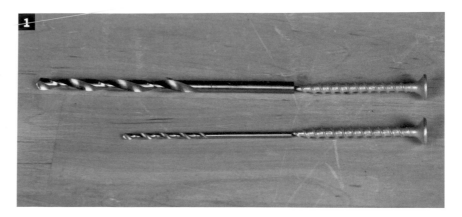

The drills needed for clearance and pilot holes.

Drill a clearance hole in the first piece of wood so the screw will fit.

Then drill a pilot hole in the second piece.

The finished clearance hole, with countersink, and pilot holes.

The pieces will pull together tightly when screwed.

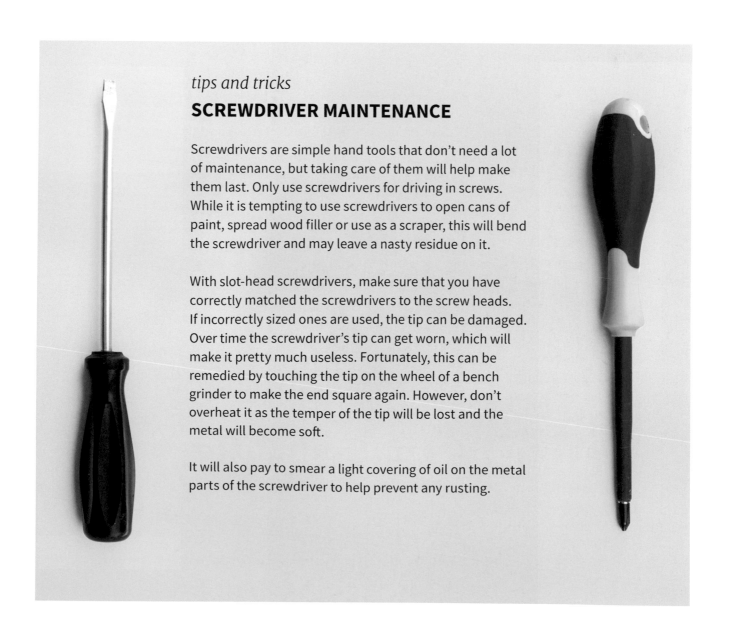

tips and tricks

SCREWDRIVER MAINTENANCE

Screwdrivers are simple hand tools that don't need a lot of maintenance, but taking care of them will help make them last. Only use screwdrivers for driving in screws. While it is tempting to use screwdrivers to open cans of paint, spread wood filler or use as a scraper, this will bend the screwdriver and may leave a nasty residue on it.

With slot-head screwdrivers, make sure that you have correctly matched the screwdrivers to the screw heads. If incorrectly sized ones are used, the tip can be damaged. Over time the screwdriver's tip can get worn, which will make it pretty much useless. Fortunately, this can be remedied by touching the tip on the wheel of a bench grinder to make the end square again. However, don't overheat it as the temper of the tip will be lost and the metal will become soft.

It will also pay to smear a light covering of oil on the metal parts of the screwdriver to help prevent any rusting.

HOW TO USE A DRILL

The hand drill is becoming more of a hard-to-find tool these days as it has been mostly replaced by the mains power or cordless version. However, it is still a useful tool to have in your toolbox. Hand drills require a firm grip and some practice to master, but once this is attained you will find yourself enjoying drilling by hand.

Drill techniques

A decent set of drills is a good investment. The drill has a chuck on the end and that is what holds the drill bit (see page 29). This is adjustable in size so you can drill a wide range of hole sizes. The chuck has jaws that close together when the main part of the body is rotated and these jaws are what grips the drill bit. Rotate the chuck body by hand until the jaws close on the drill bit, then using a chuck key, tighten the jaws onto the bit. To release the drill bit, reverse the process.

Drill holes in wood to use for dowel joints (see page 66) or for pilot and clearance holes for screwing (see page 48). Position the drill where you want to drill a hole and start rotating the crank handle, clockwise, which will spin the drill bit. Smaller diameter drill bits will be easier to spin when cutting into the wood so it may be a good idea to drill a small hole first and work up through drill sizes to the size hole you want. Hold the drill upright and then the hole it drills will be straight in the wood.

Tighten the drill bit into the drill's chuck using a chuck key.

Hold the hand drill firmly and keep upright for precise hole drilling.

tips and tricks
PRECISE DRILLING

A useful tip if you need to drill a precise depth hole, for a dowel for example, is to wrap a piece of tape around the drill bit at the distance from the end that you want the hole to be in depth. Drill until the tape touches the surface of the wood and your hole is then the correct depth.

Wrap a piece of tape around the drill bit at the depth you want the hole to be.

Drill the hole until the tape meets the surface of the wood and your hole is now exactly the depth you want it to be.

Power tools
In this basic woodworking book, power tools have mainly been avoided as they can be an expensive investment. It is delightful to master the use of hand tools, which give you a deeper insight into how wood works.

However, there are some power tools that we would recommend that might be the next step once your interest in woodworking has been nurtured. There are four tools that could speed up your work and they are the circular saw, the jigsaw, the power drill and the sander. There are unique skills needed to use these power tools too, but most of the basic information for using hand tools will apply to power tools as well.

HOW TO USE A CHISEL

Having a selection of chisels in your toolbox will pay dividends as a chisel is a versatile tool, but must be used with care. The very sharp edge is designed to shave away slices of wood in a controlled way.

Types of chisel

The plain- and the bevel-edge chisel (see page 27) are probably the most likely types of chisel to have in your toolbox for basic woodworking. The bevel-edge chisel is well worth the investment as the bevel edge enables the chisel to get into small areas when space is tight. They come in different widths and a ¾in (19mm) wide one will probably be the most used chisel as it will be the most versatile one. If you buy a good-quality chisel and look after it by keeping it in a safe place to prevent it rusting or getting damaged, and occasionally sharpen it when needed, it will last a lifetime.

Using a chisel

When cutting, hold the chisel so you have a good firm grip on its handle. Hold it in such a way that your fingers never come close to its sharp edge as it will cut you badly if you allow it to. When you cut the wood, always cut with the grain, as cutting against the grain will cause the chisel to dig in and split the wood. Most cuts are made with the bevel up, while heavier cuts may require the chisel to be used bevel down.

Cutting recesses

A simple and useful task for a chisel is to cut the recess for a hinge or door strike plate. First mark where the recess needs to be. This can be done by placing the hinge or strike plate on the wood in exactly the position it needs to sit, then mark round it with a sharp pencil. An alternative is to use a knife to make the mark and this will give a cut edge to work from.

Strike a few pencil lines over the waste part so it is obvious what needs to be removed. Place the chisel in the marks and strike the end of it with a mallet to cut deeper into the wood and establish the boundaries of the recess.

A small set of bevel-edge chisels. Wooden mallets are the best choice for tapping the end. You will also needs a sharpening stone for the edge when the chisel gets blunt.

Mark the extents of the hinge's recess either with a pencil or knife: first the ends…

…then the width…

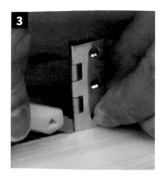

…then the thickness.

Use the combination square to extend the cut mark.

Use a pencil to mark the waste area. This makes it obvious which part of the wood needs removing.

Hold the chisel on the cut marks and tap its end with a mallet to create deeper cuts.

Cut chips with the chisel along the length of the recess.

Clear out the chips; they will just flick out.

Make sure that you don't cut too deep. Then, hold the chisel securely in the mark on the long front edge, start to pare out the chips you have just created. Once removed, you can use the chisel in a slicing action to remove the remaining wood and create a smooth and accurate recess.

Cut across the grain to remove more waste wood.

Then using a firm grip on the chisel, shave thinner slices.

For an even finer finish, use the chisel bevel down and lengthways with the grain, to shave the recess and create a smooth and accurate finish.

Check the hinge is a good fit in the recess then screw it in place.

Sharpening a chisel

Keeping a sharp edge on your chisel will make sure you get nice smooth cuts but will also make it more controllable as it will cut through the wood more easily. You will need a sharpening stone for the job and, if you are using an oil stone, some cutting oil. A small amount is applied on the stone. Place the flat side of the chisel on the stone and rub this a couple of times on the surface to make sure it is flat.

Then turn the chisel over and lay the bevel edge on the surface of the stone and slide it around in a figure-of-eight movement. Make sure that you keep the bevel edge of the chisel at the same angle all the time you are moving it. This will ensure that you achieve a flat cutting edge on the chisel. This is not an aggressive procedure and little pressure should be applied; you let the movement

on the abrasive stone do all the work. Sharpening the bevel will produce a small burr, which, when removed, will give a sharp edge again.

There are reams of information available on sharpening techniques, but this is all you need to complete the basic process for giving your chisels a sharp edge.

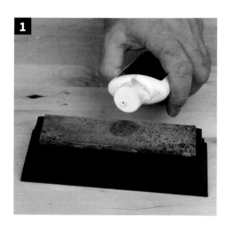

A sharpening stone and cutting oil is what you need to keep a sharp edge on your chisels.

Hone the bevel edge of your chisel by holding it at the angle shown and move it evenly all over the surface of the stone.

Place the back of the chisel on the stone and rub it on the stone until it is flat.

tips and tricks
SHARPENING STONE OPTIONS

Like any abrasive system, sharpening stones can be obtained in different grit options; some even have two grits in one, with a coarse grit one side and a fine grit the other. When a blade has become really blunt you will need to use a coarse stone to reinstate the cutting edge and then a fine stone to hone a sharp edge on it.

HOW TO USE A HAND PLANE

The hand plane is really just a thin, wide chisel, called a blade, held in a manageable handle and used as a wood-smoothing tool.

Hand planes come in many sizes. These two will be the most used ones.

The plane's blade protrudes slightly below the base of the plane and that is how it cuts shavings.

Always lay a hand plane on its side as its blade protrudes below the base and could get damaged if the plane is set down on its base.

The action of the hand plane

The most useful types are the smoothing plane and the block plane (see page 30). To use the plane, the blade is held at an angle and protrudes slightly below the face of the bottom of the plane. When you push the plane across the surface of a piece of wood, the cutting edge of the blade cuts into the wood and produces a shaving. The precise thickness that the knife protrudes through the base then passes through a gap in the bottom of the plane. This process cuts accurate shavings from the wood and produces a smooth surface. The longer the planes are, the straighter the surfaces they will produce.

tips and tricks
BUYING OLD HAND PLANES

If you go to flea markets it is likely that you will see old hand planes being sold. Don't dismiss them because they are rusty; they are probably made from better-quality metal than a cheap hand plane from a DIY store. Remove the rust with fine sandpaper, sharpen the blade, and a light coat of oil over the tool will make it look like new.

Hand plane techniques

Holding the plane correctly and adopting a good stance will greatly enhance the finish you will achieve. Hold the handle in your power hand (that is, left or right, depending on your handedness) and the other hand on the knob to enable you to guide the plane. Pushing the plane while applying some downward pressure will produce satisfying ribbons of wood as it is sliced off your work. If you have a problem pushing the plane it is probably because the blade is set to cut too deep or is blunt. If this is the case, adjust the depth and try again or sharpen the blade.

One of the things we often use a hand plane for is to cut off the sharp edges on a workpiece. Simply hold the plane at a 45° angle to the corner and run it along the length of the work. This produces a consistent small, chamfered edge that looks professional. Sharpening the planer's knife is very similar to sharpening a chisel except you have to remove the knife from the plane's body and remember how to put it back again.

Hold the hand plane correctly to produce fine shavings.

A small plane is useful for quickly shaving the edge off workpieces.

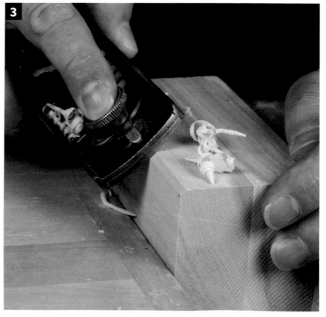

The bevel is visually pleasing and cutting it by hand is very satisfying.

HOW TO USE A CLAMP

The whole subject of clamping is a huge one, but for our purposes we are using some simple clamps that are versatile and readily available. The basic rules of clamping are pretty much the same for all types of clamp; they hold the pieces of work together while the glue dries.

Protecting your work

Bar clamps are used for many types of work (see page 34). All of them feature a pair of jaws that close to clamp workpieces. As clamps can exert a lot of pressure you should be careful not to damage your workpieces when using them. The clamp's jaws are probably going to be harder than the wood they are clamping, so pads need to be placed between them and the wood. Small pieces of softwood can be made into pads and it is useful to keep these handy as they can be used time and time again.

Clamps should not be over-tightened, but if you find the joint not pulling together easily there is probably a reason for it. There may be too much glue or the joint has not been cut correctly.

These two simple types of bar clamps are versatile, easily available and inexpensive.

These clamps are easily adjusted for different lengths with their quick-release lever, then tightened using the T-bar.

Always use pads made of softwood to protect your work from the jaws of the clamps.

Position of clamps

Position clamps carefully so they pull a joint together evenly. If a clamp's jaws are placed at an angle to a joint it will pull unevenly and the joint will not pull together successfully. When you have completed your project, make sure you inspect the clamps and clean off any glue that has dripped onto them. Excess glue could prevent the clamps from working properly the next time.

When clamping joints, make sure the clamps are aligned squarely, otherwise the joint will not pull together properly.

When the clamps are aligned correctly, they will pull the joint together evenly.

tips and tricks

A VICE CAN BE A USEFUL CLAMPING TOOL

It is unlikely that you will have a bench with a built-in vice like the one featured in this book, so you may want to buy an inexpensive vice that you can clamp to your existing bench. The one shown here has large flat jaws especially designed for woodworking. When holding wood in the vice jaws to cut or sand the workpiece, make sure that you use wooden pads to prevent the jaws from damaging the wood.

HOW TO MEASURE AND MARK

In woodworking, you need to measure and mark lines to know where to make cuts in the wood. Measuring accurately is extremely important, because if done incorrectly your cut will be made in the wrong place and the piece of wood is likely to end up in the scrap bin.

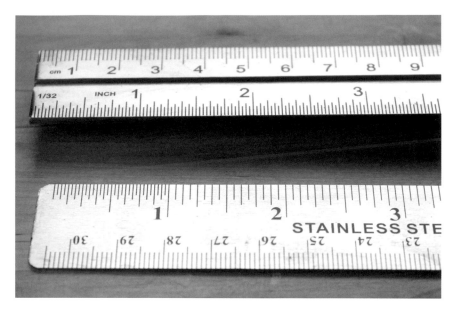

A measuring tool using both metric and imperial systems.

Steel rule

Of all the measuring devices available, the steel rule is the one to start with (see page 32). A steel rule is more durable than a plastic one and it is easier to see the increments of measure. As we have seen, steel rules may use the metric system or the imperial system. If you choose one with both systems on them, you have a choice. The hardness and flexibility of the steel means it can be cut against with a knife without damaging it. It can also be gently curved, set on a piece of wood and used as a tool for marking arcs with a pencil.

The three most popular measuring devices: the steel rule, the combination square and the tape measure.

Tape measure

The next most popular measuring device used for making long measurements is the tape measure (see page 32). It also features different or a mix of measuring systems and is extremely portable as the flexible tape retracts into the body on the tape. A lock on the tape can hold a length of tape outside the body so it isn't continually trying to retract.

The tape is very thin, with measuring increments printed on the tape so there is very little deflection. This reduces the need to keep your eye at right angles to the tape when marking with a pencil. The right-angled hook at the end of the tape measure slides back and forth exactly the thickness of its end, so that when you are measuring against an object it pushes into the tape – and when measuring from the edge of an object, the end hooks over it and pulls away from the tape. This is a function of the tape measure that ensures accurate measurement in both situations. However, over time the end can wear out and make the tape inaccurate so you can check to see by aligning it against a ruler to make sure the measurements match.

The hooked end of the tape measure moves. Pushed-in is for measuring inside measurements.

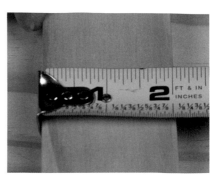

Pulled-out is for measuring external measurements.

tips and tricks

USING A KNIFE LINE AS A MARKER

If you are going to saw along a pencil line, a handy tip to remember is to use a knife to cut the marked line into the wood. Align your saw so its kerf cuts on the waste side of the knife line. As you have pre-cut the grain fibres of the wood with the sharp knife, you will get a cleaner edge because the coarse teeth of the saw won't be tearing the grain.

A knife can also be used for marking.

This knife-cut mark will give a clean edge when sawing.

Combination square

There is often a need to measure and mark at right angles to the edge of a piece of wood, and the tool to use for this is the combination square (see page 32). The combination square has more functions than a traditional square and has measuring increments along its rule. The rule can be slid in relation to its body's square edge and this makes it easier to set distances from the workpiece edge. The 45°-angle edge on the tool is useful for marking mitres, for example, and the built-in spirit level bubble helps keep the surface level when being used.

The first thing to do before using a new square is to check to make sure it is actually square. Place the tool's square edge on the edge of a piece of wood and draw a line along the rule. Then turn the tool around and position the rule on the line you have previously drawn and draw a new line. If the two lines are parallel then your square is true and can be used. If the lines are not parallel then your square is bent and should not be used. It is a good idea to check this periodically as it can be easy to drop the tool and knock it out of square.

The rule of the combination square can be set in different positions in the body, while positions are marked on the end of the rule.

To check your square is square, mark a line with the combination square.

Then flip it round and check that the rule lines up with the line you drew.

Marking with a pencil

Use a pencil to make marks where you need them, for drilling holes perhaps, or to draw a line across the wood at right angles to its edge.

Using a mid-range hardness lead such as HB means the mark you make is thin, but visible. Make sure your pencil is sharp and when using it against the rule, make sure that your eye is at right angles to the rule so the pencil marks exactly the measuring increment you want to use. If your eye is off to one side the thickness of the rule will show the pencil lined up on an increment, but the mark it makes will be to one side.

If you are marking multiple pieces of wood where a cut or hole needs to be in the same position on all of them, it is a good idea to clamp them together and mark across all of them with a pencil. This ensures that there won't be an error when measuring.

There is often the need to mark circles or arcs and instead of investing in curve-drawing templates you can use household items, such as jar lids, instead. You may have to hunt for a while to find one the right size.

Choose a good pencil that will make a visible line. Here is a carpenter's pencil and a regular pencil; either of these will do a good job.

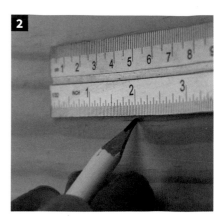

If you are to one side of the rule and make a mark…

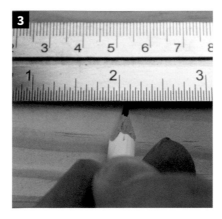

…when you check the mark from above it will not be in line with the ruler's mark. This is due to the thickness of the ruler.

Ensure that your eye is directly over the rule to get an accurate measurement.

Marking multiple pieces that are clamped together.

Household items, such as lids, can be used for marking arcs or circles.

HOW TO APPLY GLUE

Applying glue is an important skill to master. Glue is most commonly used in conjunction with a woodworking joint, and the glue reinforces the holding power of the joint. However, there are some instances where glue alone is used.

Types of glue

We will just use the typical woodworker's white or yellow PVA glue as this is readily available in most DIY stores and is a well proven and inexpensive glue for most woodworking purposes. Glue containers come in different sizes and some have a pointed nozzle and some have a flat one. Most nozzles are self-sealing these days, which will help prolong the life of your glue.

Edge gluing

For joining two pieces of wood together along their edge without a mechanical joint, such as a tongue and groove, it is recommended that the wood is thick enough to ensure there is a good surface area to be glued. This is also a way of bulking up wood to sizes that you may not have or be able to buy.

Apply the glue along the length of one of the edges in a squiggly line, making sure to apply a good amount of glue. Spread the glue and place the two edges together, on a flat surface, and slide the pieces of wood back and forth a little. This will help spread the glue evenly and after a few strokes the two surfaces will adhere together. This is called a rub joint and you may not even need clamps to hold the boards together.

Edge-gluing multiple pieces

Edge-gluing more than two pieces of wood together gets a bit more complicated as there are many pieces to juggle. Line up your pieces of wood on a flat surface and make sure that you have bar clamps to hand. Use the previous technique of applying the glue in a squiggly line along one edge of all the pieces of wood, but then assemble all the mating edges together as close as you can and then clamp them all together. You can put paper on the bench to help protect it from excess glue. If there is a tendency for the pieces of wood to bend apart on their edges you can wedge pieces of wood under the clamp to stop them springing while they are being clamped together.

You need to think about how much glue to apply – you will want enough to spread evenly in the edge joint, but not so much so that it oozes out excessively either side of the joint. Too much glue makes cleaning up much more difficult.

Glue containers have different nozzle types. Some nozzles are pointed for getting into small recesses while others are wide for spreading.

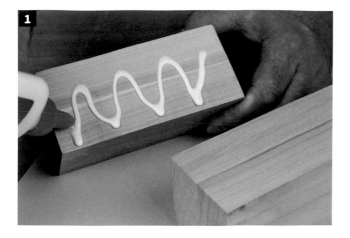

Apply the glue in a squiggly line.

Spread the glue over the surface with a flat tool.

Push the pieces of wood together.

Rub the pieces of wood back and forth.

Finally, they will stick tightly together.

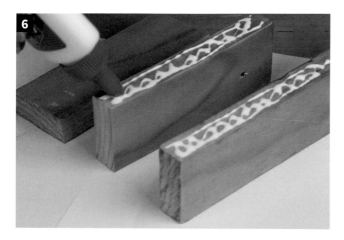

On multiple pieces, run a squiggly line of glue on all the mating edges.

Clamp the edges together. The glue should ooze out a little, but not too much.

Apply glue into the dowel hole.

Spread glue all around the hole with a nail.

The glue will run up a dowel with flutes.

Gluing joints

Adding glue to a joint will hold it together and make it secure from coming apart. The woodworking joint does a great job of aligning the parts of wood being joined, but without glue it would only rely on friction to hold it together. The correct application of glue can make the joint stronger as well as making the clean-up afterwards either hard or easy.

Using dowels

Dowels are a commonly used and are a relatively simple method of joining wood together. Holes are drilled in the mating pieces and the dowel inserted in the holes. The technique here is to apply the glue into the holes using a glue container with a smallish size tip. Place the tip of the glue container into the dowel hole about midway down the hole and squeeze some glue into it, then, with a little stick or nail, spread the glue all round the hole. If there is too much glue, just pull it out on the stick and wipe it off on a rag. Repeat this on all the holes that will receive a dowel.

Being a liquid, glue cannot be compressed, so the dowel hole should be a little deeper than the dowel is long. Making the hole longer gives the excess glue somewhere to go. If the glue has nowhere to go it will hold the joint apart or if pressure with clamps is applied it can crack the wood. Tap the dowel into the hole. If your dowel is a store-bought joint dowel, it will most likely have flutes running along its length. These flutes are to allow glue to run up them and spread evenly; they will also help to eliminate the glue locking the dowel. If you are using smooth dowel you can run a small saw cut along its length to do the same thing.

Once you have the dowels inserted in their holes use clamps to pull the wood pieces together and leave them there until the glue has dried.

CLEARING GLUE FROM JOINTS

When gluing joints such as a mortise and tenon together, you will probably see glue oozing from the shoulder of the joint. If the correct amount of glue is used there will be just a small bead and this is best removed with a chisel when the glue is almost dry.

Glue will ooze out of a joint in a small bead if the correct amount of glue is used.

Using a chisel, when the glue is nearly dry, cut the bead one way.

Now cut off the bead for a clean internal shoulder.

HOW TO SAND

Getting a smooth finish on wood will make your projects look great and the way to achieve this is to sand the wood with sandpaper. It is tempting to use a power sander, especially if you have a lot of sanding to do. However, it is good training to learn good hand-sanding skills before moving on to the powered alternative.

Sanding grits

Sandpaper comes in different grits. The grit refers to how coarse the abrasive particles are that coat the paper. The coarser the particles, the more aggressive the sandpaper will be. Coarse paper is quick and rough, whereas fine paper is slow and smooth.

Using coarse sandpaper

On shop bought wood, the surface of planed wood has shallow scalloped marks left by the rotary action of the wood yard's planer cutters and after handling wood there will also be some slight dings and dents. You should use coarse sandpaper such as 80 grit to quickly remove these imperfections. Be careful though, as you can sand too much using coarse grit.

Use a flat wooden block that comfortably fits your hand, but as large as you can manage, then sand the corners of the block. Wrap a piece of sandpaper around the block and pin it in place or simply hold it with your fingers. You can buy pre-made sanding blocks with clamps to hold the sandpaper, but homemade ones work just as well.

Rub the block and sandpaper over the surface of your wood, making sure to only sand along the wood's grain. If you sand across the grain the abrasive on the sandpaper will tear the wood's fibres and leave coarse marks. These will be very difficult to remove and will be extremely noticeable if you use a stain on the wood as it will show darker in these cross-grain marks. The only time to sand across the grain is on the end grain, where the marks will be less pronounced.

Working through the grits

When you have sanded all the imperfections from the wood, you can sand with less coarse sandpaper. To achieve a sanded finish that is ideal for applying a stain and finish, aim to use 180 grit as the final sandpaper. Use a sequence of 80, 100, 120, 150 then 180 grit to achieve this (80 grit is the coarsest and 180 grit is the finest). Although this is a bit time consuming the results will pay off.

Sandpaper comes in different grits, depending on how fast you want to remove wood and how smooth a finish you want.

Marks on planed wood need sanding off.

To sand a flat surface, use a conveniently sized block of wood with sandpaper folded round it.

Sand in the direction of the grain to ensure the best finish possible.

This is one of the few times to sand across the grain as this space is on the end grain.

Work gradually through the grits of sandpaper until the last one is the finest one you want.

tips and tricks
FOLDING SANDPAPER

For quickly sanding off sharp edges, curves or difficult places, use sandpaper folded into manageable sizes to hold in your hand and rub over the edge to make them smooth. Folding a sheet of sandpaper in half gives you greater efficiency as when the face of sandpaper you are using becomes dull and clogged you simply refold the sandpaper to expose a clean face.

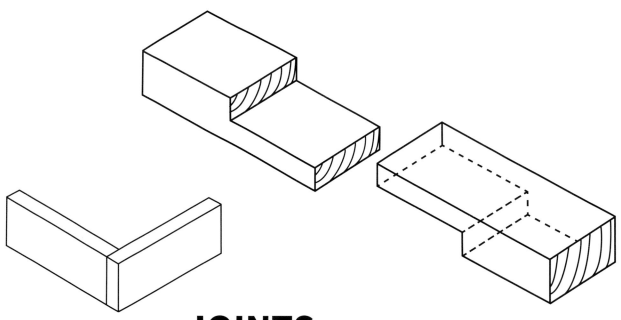

JOINTS

Wood is held together using joints. Some joints are simple and others complex, but they are all a woodworking challenge. The type of joint you use will depend on the item you are creating. The joints selected here are ones that are easily made by the beginner but still retain good functionality.

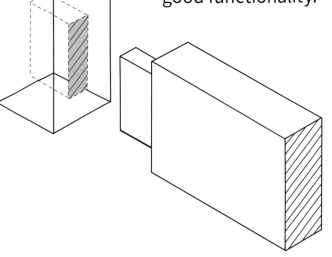

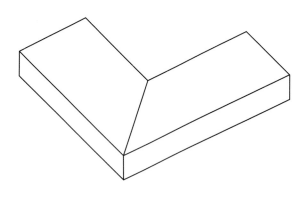

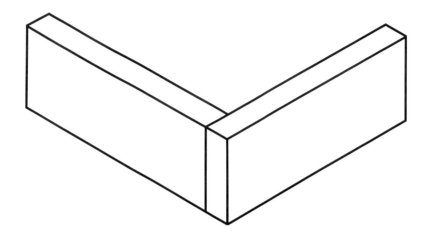

BUTT JOINTS

The butt joint may be a simple joint, but there is still some accurate measuring and cutting to be done to create it. The butt joint is two pieces of wood butted together at a 90° angle. As there is no physical joint structure it simply relies on the glue and nails or screws to hold it together. When assembled it can be a strong joint, best used for utility items such as a toolbox.

Marking, cutting and joining

The pieces of wood used in this joint first need to be cut to length. If you are making a box, you need to consider which pieces of wood go inside the other pieces. Cut these pieces shorter than your required length by twice the thickness of the wood to ensure that the finished box is the correct size. The ends need to be sawn square in both directions or the joint won't hold at all, so this is a good sawing exercise.

Start by making a line across the wood and round the edges, then with the wood held firmly, saw the end off. Take care to let the saw do the work and the resulting cut will be a nice square.

Place one piece of wood on the end of the other; you can glue here if you want, then hammer the nails in the end. They can be about 3in (75mm) apart, but use as many as you think will be needed. If you are using a nail with a head make sure you are careful to hammer it so it is just flush with the surface of the wood and the hammer's head does not leave bruise marks. If you are using lost head nails, drive them below the surface with a punch and fill the recesses.

The ends of the wood need sawing square, so mark a pencil line on them across their face.

Now continue the lines around the edges.

Hold the wood firmly and line up the edge of the saw blade on the pencil line. Saw carefully until it is cut all the way through the wood.

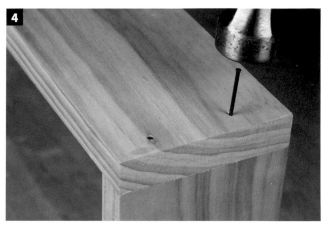

Place one piece of wood on the other at 90° with edges aligned. Add glue if needed, then hammer nails through the grain on one piece and into the end grain on the other.

If you are using lost head nails, drive their heads slightly below the surface.

The finished butt joint now only needs the nail recesses to be filled to finish.

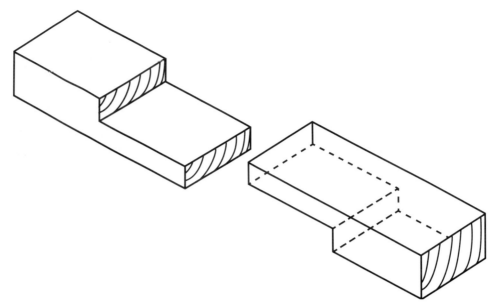

HALF-LAP JOINTS

The half-lap joint is a simple joint, but one that will help the beginner to learn accurate marking and cutting. This is a versatile joint although it is mostly used for making frames for simple cabinet doors. The joint is strong when just glued but it can be nailed, screwed or dowelled together to increase its strength.

The half-lap joint can be made in different variations depending on where in a frame it might be used: a cross joint, a T-joint and a corner joint. All of these may be needed in the construction of cabinet doors. Cutting the variants is virtually the same, apart from the cross joint. The most important thing to remember is to mark and cut accurately and to take your time. To show the different joint variations, they have been cut on the same piece of wood but in your application, you will cut them where needed.

Measuring and marking

The first step is to measure and mark the width of the joint on the face of the mating pieces of wood where you want the joint to be positioned. Use a sharp pencil to create a fine line, and on the T-joint place the mark so that there is a little extra length on the ends of the wood. These long ends

are sanded off after the joint is glued together and ensures that there is enough wood at the end of the joint. You need to extend the pencil lines across the width of the wood using the square, then mark the lines around the edge of the wood.

Use the sliding rule of the combination square to find the halfway point of the wood's thickness. Measure first, then set the end of the rule to the line and mark from either side of the wood to ensure that you have got the exact halfway point. You now need to mark the extents of the joint on all the pieces of wood. If you mark diagonal lines across the area that will be cut away, this helps ensure you are cutting in the right place as well as visualize what the finished joint will look like.

Use a square and knife to cut the lines on the faces and edges, which will ensure that you get a sharp corner when sawing. The saw will sit against these lines if there is a small 'V' cut with a chisel on the waste side of the line. With a sharp chisel, gently push at an angle slightly away from the line on the waste side and create a 'V'. Take care not to push too hard or you will cut past the line and ruin your work. Cut a 'V' groove on the waste side of all the joints you are cutting and you are ready to start cutting the joints.

Mark the width of the wood on the face of its mating piece with a sharp pencil. On the T-joint leave a little extra length for sanding off when the joint is complete.

Mark the cross joints at a midway position where they are needed.

Extend the lines across the wood.

Repeat this for all the pieces of wood.

Continue the line on the face around the wood onto the edge.

Measure and mark the halfway point of the wood's thickness on the edge of the wood.

Double check that you have marked the centre point correctly by setting the end of the square to the line and checking from one side…

…and then the other. If correct, continue to mark the centre line on all the joints.

Still using the square, now extend the width lines to the centre lines.

Draw diagonal lines to make it clear what wood needs removing.

Cut the lines with a knife to ensure a clean edge when sawing.

Using a sharp chisel, carefully cut a 'V' groove on the waste side of the line for the saw to run against.

Cut a 'V' groove on all of the marked joints.

Cutting the joint

Place the wood in a vice to keep it steady and position the blade of a fine-tooth saw in the 'V' groove against the marked and cut edge. A seasoned woodworker will use a tenon saw, but good results can be obtained using a saw without a spine. However, be careful to use a gentle sawing action so that the blade doesn't bind and flex.

Push forward with the saw to start cutting and use long strokes with the whole length of the blade to give the best cut. Don't be tempted to force the blade; just let the teeth cut their way through the wood. Make sure you only cut to the marked midway point; you will need to look at the side of the wood that is away from you to make sure that you have cut to the depth on both sides. Saw the extents of the joints on all the pieces of wood and then on the cross joints make a few saw cuts along the joint to the depth of the joint. Make the cuts a small distance apart, but it isn't critical how far or how many; you just need a few saw cuts to help create the joint. The reason for this will become clear after you have finished all the sawing.

Place the edge of a fine-tooth saw in the 'V' groove, push the saw and cut to the midway point on both sides of the wood.

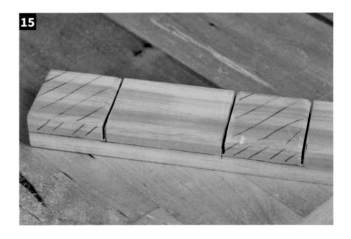

Saw the extents of the joints on all the pieces of wood.

Saw more cuts along the length of the cross joints. The reason for these cuts will be shown later.

tips and tricks
USING HALF-LAP JOINTS

The simplicity of half-lap joints means that they reveal end grain on both sides of the joint. Avoid using the joint where showing grain might not be the look that is wanted. Use them on workshop cabinet door frames, bench leg frames and internal frames for furniture, for example.

Now you can start on the corner or T-joints. As these are on the ends of the wood they can be cut with a saw. Hold the wood with one end in a vice and saw along the grain on the waste side of the line until the cross cut is reached and the waste piece is cut away. Repeat this sawing procedure on all the end joints. Now come back to the cross joints and get the sharp chisel ready. All the cross cuts made earlier can now be knocked out with the chisel. They pop out easily as they are only short and the grain easily splits. With the wood pieces out of the way, use the chisel to start cleaning out the joint.

Use a gentle slicing action with the chisel to shave out the waste wood and achieve a smooth bottom of the joint. Also check the width and if needed, trim wood off the ends too so that the joint will fit together. Care is needed so as not to cut too much away. It is good practice to trial-fit the joint as you go and if the faces do not line up, gently slice more wood out until it is a good fit. Time spent here will pay dividends – a tight-fitting joint is a strong joint.

When all the joints have been cut you can assemble the joint. Shown here are a cross joint, a T-joint and a corner joint, all of which can be used to make cabinet door frames.

17

Place the wood upright in the vice and saw with the blade on the waste side of the line.

18

Start sawing carefully to make sure you cut along the line. Let the saw's teeth do the cutting and do not force the saw.

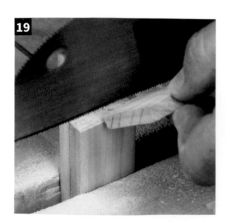

19

Continue sawing until the cross cut is reached and the waste piece falls away.

20

The end joint looks a bit rough, but the chisel will clean it up.

21

Using a chisel and mallet, knock out the small pieces in the cross joint.

The chisel is now used with a slicing action to clean out the joint.

Test the joint and to see how it fits. There is probably more chiselling to be done at this stage.

If the joint is tight, trim the ends with the chisel. Take care not to cut too much.

Trial-fit the joint again and this time it shows that more wood needs to come out of the bottom of the joint.

Here are three variants of the half-lap joint: the cross joint…

…the T-joint…

…and the corner joint.

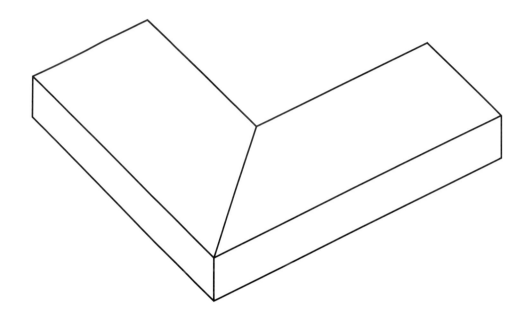

MITRE JOINTS

The mitre joint is essentially a decorative joint that will hide the end grain on the corners of an assembled wooden item. The mitre is made by cutting equal angles on the ends of two pieces of wood that will create a joint with twice that angle when put together. A mitre joint that is simply glued together can be made stronger by using nails or screws to hold the two pieces together. You could even introduce another joint within it, such as using a dowel, to give it more strength.

The mitre joint can be used in a number of applications; the one most often seen would be for picture frames where the ends are cut at 45° to create a 90° joint, which we will make here, but once you start looking they are everywhere. Look at the moulding trim around doors and windows, the edge around a table top or kitchen countertop, the drawer box in a cabinet or even the corner joints of a small jewellery box.

This deceptively simple joint relies on the accuracy of measuring and cutting to ensure a perfect joint. The 45° angle has to be exact or the 90° angle will be off by twice the error of the 45° cut. This will then multiply the error all around the frame, if that is what you are making. The cut also has to be at 90° to the surface of the wood or the joints will be angled vertically too. There are reasons you might actually want to alter these angles and create something called a compound mitre, but that is for more advanced purposes than we are covering here.

Hold the workpiece tightly against the fence of the mitre box and make the cut with the saw in the 45° slot.

Cutting the mitre

The most successful technique to hand cut mitres is to use a mitre box. These are inexpensive jigs that have slots in them at 45° and 90° angles for a saw blade to run in and pretty much ensure that you cut an accurate mitre. Hold the mitre box firmly; We use the bench vice but you can also clamp it to the bench. Place the piece of wood inside the mitre box against the furthest edge so that the cutting action of the saw will push the workpiece towards the upright of the box and keep it firmly in place. You can hold the wood with a clamp if you like, but as you are sawing gently it is also possible to hold the wood with your non-sawing hand. There is a slight tendency for the wood to creep towards the saw blade but a firm grip of the workpiece will counteract this.

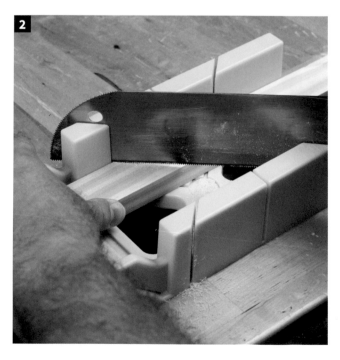

The adjacent piece of work is cut with the saw in the opposite 45° slot of the mitre box.

Align the saw blade with a line you have marked on the nearest side of the wood and push the saw forwards to start the cut. Continue sawing, making sure that the saw's teeth do the work, until you have sawn through the wood and the first part of the mitre is complete. Now line up your wood with the 45° angle on the other side of the mitre box, position your saw against your marked line and make this mating cut. Making the cut in different directions on the two pieces of wood ensures that the saw cuts the face of the wood on both pieces and any tearout is on the bottom of both.

Once the second cut is made, you can place the two 45° angles together and check to see if the finished angle is 90°. If not, then your sawing might be off and you will need to practise some more. There is also the possibility that the mitre box is worn and needs replacing. If the mitre is successful, continue cutting all your mitres ready for putting together.

Making the cuts in opposite directions makes sure that the face of the wood of both pieces get a clean cut with the tearout on the underside.

When the mating 45° faces are put together the resulting joint should be 90°; this is easily checked with a square.

If the finished angle isn't 90° then you may need to practise more sawing or check that the mitre box isn't worn. You can see the underside tearout on the piece on the right.

If the strength of the mitre is not critical, simply glue the faces and wrap masking tape around it. The result will be fairly strong with just the glue.

For a stronger joint, tap a small nail in the corner so it holds both pieces while the glue sets. Knock the sharp point off the nail to stop the wood splitting.

Holding and finishing the joint

Once a mitre is cut it can be a difficult joint to hold together while the glue dries as the angles make it difficult for a regular clamp to hold. A simple technique for achieving this is to wrap a strip of masking tape around the corner of the joint. If you are just putting a mitre on two pieces, then you may need to hold the mitre together on the other side of the masking tape. It is more normal to be making a four-sided frame, in which case all the pieces will hold together when the last piece of tape is applied.

It is common practice for picture frames or table edging to have a small nail hammered into the corner to hold the frame together. It is a good idea to make the sharp point of the nail blunt (see page 43) to stop the wood splitting as the nail is being put in close to the edge. A nail punch is also useful to knock the head of the nail below the surface of the wood. The recess can then be filled with wood filler.

Not every mitre is going to be perfect and a good tip here is to run a round tool up and down the corner of the mitre to round it over and hide any discrepancies created while sawing. This is called 'burnishing the edge'.

Burnish the edge of the mitre to hide any imperfections. Slightly round over the point by gently rubbing with a screwdriver's shaft.

This will hide any gaps that may be left after sawing.

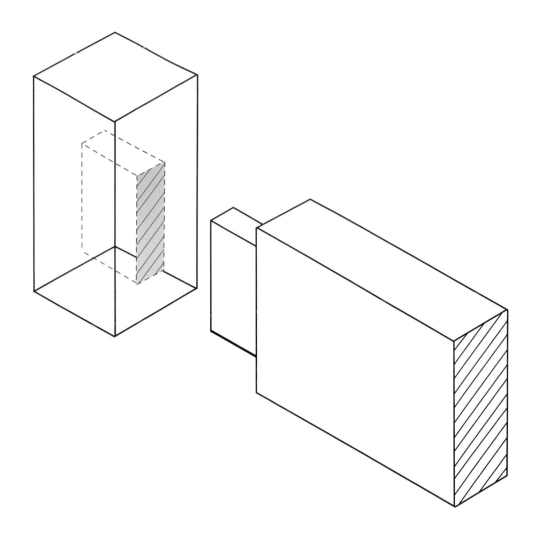

MORTISE AND TENON JOINTS

The mortise and tenon joint is probably one you have heard of as it has been used for thousands of years. It is essentially a peg in a hole where the tenon is the peg and the mortise is the hole. There are many variations on the joint but two of them are the simplest and strongest.

The 'stub tenon' is the version made here. This is where the tenon is stopped inside the wood. The 'through tenon' is where the tenon goes all the way through the wood. This is done so that the mortise is easier to cut and the tenon end can also be used as a decorative effect. The mortise and tenon is a joint commonly used in making furniture frames because it is strong, accurate and in its simplest form relatively easy to create.

Marking the joint

With this joint it is important to make sure that the joint is positioned in the same place relative to the face of both pieces of wood, so when the joint is assembled the faces of both pieces are flush. To help recognize the faces a mark is drawn lightly in pencil on them. This could just be a squiggle but there is a woodworking standard for this mark in the form of a curl and a straight. The curl is the starting point and the straight points to the common edge, and this denotes that these faces and edges are the datum to work from. In this example, it is only the face that we are interested in but it is good practice to use this style of line.

The first thing to do is to set the depth of the joint. For the stub tenon it wants to be as deep as possible, but stop short of the other side, leaving enough wood so that it retains strength. A through tenon would go all the way through and the mortise may need cutting from both sides. Mark a line on the piece of wood that will be having the tenon cut on it, at the depth you want it to be. Then extend this line all around the wood using the square.

Put face and edge marks on both pieces of wood to make sure the joint is cut in the right place.

Mark the depth you want the joint to be. This will be the shoulder of the joint.

Extend the line across the face.

Then extend it around the edge, the other edge and lastly the opposing face.

This is what will become the shoulder of the joint, which will butt up to the other piece. Now mark the position of the mortise. It needs to be the width of the tenon piece of wood minus a small distance to ensure that the shoulder of the tenon goes all round. It is common practice to set the tenon piece a distance in from the end of the wood so that when the mortise is chiselled out there is some wood on the end to prevent the wood from splitting.

This end is called a horn and is sawn off after the joint has been assembled. Now mark the extents of the tenon on both pieces to show the size of both the mortise and the tenon. The thickness of the joint is next to be marked and to make things easy We are going to make it the width of a chisel, as that is what is going to be cutting the mortise. Transfer the thickness marks all around the tenon and then along the mortise. Now you have all the lines you are going to cut to with the saw and chisel.

Now mark the width of the wood ready to calculate the width of the joint. It is good practice to leave an end on the wood that can be cut off after the joint is assembled.

The width of the joint needs to be set back from the edge to create a shoulder all around the tenon. Mark this distance on both the mortise and tenon.

The thickness of the joint is determined by the chisel that is going to cut it. Mark its width on the wood.

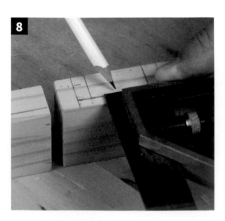

Using the depth capability of the combination square, extend these marks along both the tenon and mortise. Make sure that the face marks are on the same side.

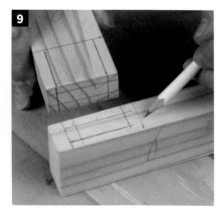

Now all the lines are marked it becomes clear where the cuts need to be made to create the joint.

Start cutting the mortise with a chisel positioned on the end. Mark and tap it to create a chop line.

Cutting the joint

Mortise Start with cutting the mortise and securely hold the piece of wood by using a vice or clamp on your bench. Place a chisel on the end mark of the mortise and tap it with the mallet to cut into the wood. Then rotate the chisel 90° and cut along the mortise line. Be careful when chopping in line with the grain as it is easy to split the wood. Cut into the other end of the mortise on the line and then along the grain again. You have now created the extents of the mortise and can start chopping out the wood. Chop into the mortise to create little blocks that will pop out, then chop into the ends of the mortise again, going a little deeper.

Continue this process until the depth of mortise has been reached. Be careful not to lever too hard with this type of chisel or it could bend or break. There are special thick mortise chisels available, but they can be purchased further down the line. Once you have cut the mortise to depth you might need to shave out the joint to make it smooth. Don't take out too much wood as it will make your joint loose.

Tenon To cut the tenon, start by placing the wood end-up in a vice, and cut along the grain with a saw. Make sure that you position the saw blade on the waste side of the line and saw down to the shoulder line on all four sides. Now secure the wood horizontally and make the cuts on the shoulder line. Make sure you take care with these cuts and that they line up all round the wood; they will be

seen so any discrepancy will make the joint look bad. The small pieces of wood that were created with the previous saw cut are released when the saw reaches the correct depth.

The tenon is now created and it may need shaving with a chisel to clean it up. Trial-fit the joint and it should be a snug fit. If it is too tight just shave some more until it is a snug fit. Your mortise and tenon is now complete and the assembled joint is a testament to your measuring, chiselling and sawing skills. However, you might need to practise cutting the joint a few times to get it right.

Rotate the chisel 90° and chop along the line, being careful not to split the wood. Chop the opposite end and back along the grain.

With the extents of the mortise now cut, chop into it to create a series of little blocks, which are easy to pop out.

Repeat the process a little at a time until the mortise is cut to depth.

Clean it out with a chisel in small shavings. Make sure not to cut out too much or the joint will be loose.

With the tenon piece of wood held securely, start sawing along the tenon's lines, making sure the saw blade is on the waste side of the line.

Saw to the shoulder line, making sure that you stop on the line or slightly before or the wrong cut will be seen.

Cut all the tenon lines to the shoulder line.

Now hold the wood in the vice horizontally and saw on the shoulder line.

The small pieces of wood created with the previous cuts will be released when the cut is the correct depth.

Saw the shoulder line all around the wood and the tenon will be revealed.

Fine-tune the joint by shaving it with a chisel, if required.

Test the fit of the joint to see if it is a snug fit; if it's too tight, shave some more wood off.

It is now ready to be pulled together to complete the mortise and tenon joint.

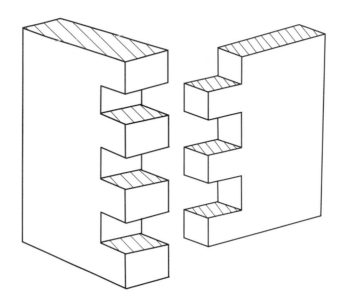

WIDE BOX JOINTS

This box joint is designed to hold the corners of a project together securely and is the ideal joint for making boxes. This version of the joint is what we are going to call a wide box joint, where the slots that interlock are more widely spaced than usual. This makes it quicker and easier to cut by hand, but it still retains its strength and looks attractive.

There are many other corner joints, such as the dovetail joint and lock mitre joint, but they require expensive machinery or advanced woodworking skills to make. The finger, comb or box joint is one corner joint where many offset slots are cut into the end of two pieces of wood that interlock like fingers. This can also be a complex joint to create due to the large number of fingers to be cut. Think of the wide box joint as an entry-level corner joint that will do what you need it to do for now, but may pique your interest to cut more complex joints in the future.

Measuring and marking

The marking of this joint is the critical part and measuring is not so important, as long as all the marking is done from a common datum. This datum is the face and edge marks that are the curl and straight lines that meet on a corner. They show where all the measuring and marking is to be done from.

Mark the faces and edges on all your pieces of wood. In this case the face is going to be the outside of the joint. Place the square ends of the pieces together, making sure that the faces and edges are on the same sides and the edges are flush with each other. Then, from the marked edge, either measure or mark in a visually pleasing location the extents of the joint on both pieces.

Using a square extend these marks all around the pieces of wood, making sure that the square is resting on a marked edge or face. Then from the square edges of the pieces extend the lines around the end of the wood. This is a joint where it is critical to diagonally mark pencil lines in the areas of wood that will be removed. Without this visual guide it is easy to make the cut in the wrong place.

Marking the face and edge is critical with this joint as it needs to be set out using a reliable datum.

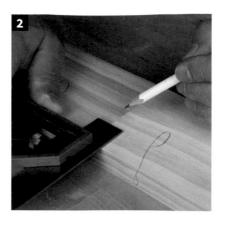

The position of the joint parts can either be measured or marked freehand, depending on what kind of look you want.

Make sure the lines are on the ends of both pieces of wood.

Mark the thickness of the wood on the ends of each piece. This determines the depth of the joint.

Extend the lines all around the wood, making sure that the square part is on the marked face or edge.

Extend the joint lines round the ends of the wood.

Draw diagonal lines on the parts to be removed. This will help to make sure the cuts are in the right place.

Cutting the joint

The secret to success with this joint is to take your time and cut with care. Make sure that the saw cuts are on the waste side of the line and chisel away waste by taking thin shavings.

Clamp the first piece of wood in the vice, or if it is a wider piece then clamp it to the side of the bench. Make the saw cuts with the grain and cut alongside the line on the waste side until the depth line is reached. Make sure to keep looking on the back side of the wood to ensure your saw cut is even both sides. Cut along all the lines and do the same on the other piece of wood. The waste wood can now be removed and the process for this differs, depending if there is clear access from an outside edge or not. For the pieces with clear access the waste wood can simply be sawn out with the regular saw and for the interior ones a different type of saw can be used.

A coping saw has a narrow blade that can be used to saw a curve. Position the saw towards one of the previous saw cuts and cut towards the end of the cut on the other side of the waste part. Coping saws are not ideal to cut square across the wood, so care must be taken to get an even cut. When the other saw cut is reached, a little curved triangle of wood is released and the coping saw blade can now be positioned in the deepest part of the cut. Now saw towards the end of the previous saw cut. This will release a slimmer, rounded triangle of wood. These two cuts may be all that is needed and any small areas of waste wood left can be shaved out with a chisel to make the bottom square. Make all the cuts needed for the complete joint and give it a trial fit. You are likely to need to shave areas of wood away to get a snug fit. Make sure to cut from the face of the wood to hide any mistakes on the inside of the joint and hopefully out of view. When you are happy with the joint it can be glued together.

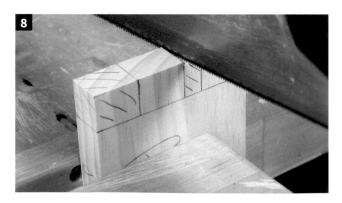

Hold the workpiece securely and saw down the parts of the joint. Make sure that the cut is on the waste side of the line.

Continue sawing carefully until the line is reached on both sides.

Saw all the end cuts.

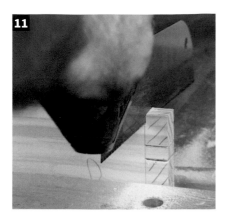

Now start removing the waste parts and saw across the grain of accessible parts first.

The waste part is released when the sawn cross cut reaches the end cut.

For the parts that are not accessible, use a coping saw with a thin blade that can cut around corners. Saw the first part from the outside of the top cut to the inside of the second cut.

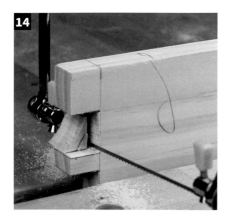

Turn the wood over and reclamp it. Saw the second part of the cut to release a small triangle of wood.

Some fine shaving of the joint will probably be required on the shoulder.

You may also need to shave the pins of the joint.

Trial-fit the joint together.

The assembled joint is a good fit.

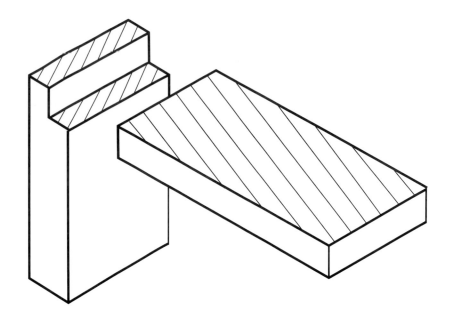

REBATE AND HOUSING JOINTS

The rebate joint, also known as a rabbet joint, is cut on the end of pieces of wood. The housing joint, also known as a dado joint, is basically a trench cut across the grain of a piece of wood into which another piece of wood is inserted. The large surface area for the gluing of the mating pieces of wood means that these joints are strong. The rebate and the housing joint can also be nailed to give them extra strength; their heads will need recessing into the wood with a punch and then the recess filled.

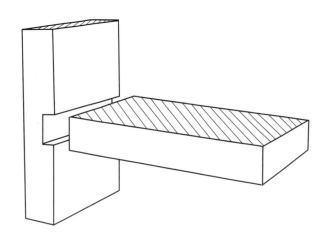

The rebate joint is similar in construction to the housing joint but it is cut on the end of a piece of wood to form a corner joint where only a little end grain shows. These joints are typically used to make cabinet boxes and shelf units where the crosspiece of wood becomes a fixed shelf. Although they are simple woodworking joints, it is essential to maintain accurate marking and cutting, and it is useful to practise learning these skills.

Marking the joints

The rebate joint on the end of the piece of wood is a simple one to mark. Ensure that the end of the piece that will have the rebate cut into it is nice and square, then place the piece of wood that will join into it on the side to be cut and flush with the end. Mark a pencil line across the wood and it will be parallel to the end. The housing joint is marked at the position that the mating piece at 90° is required. Position it on the face of the piece of wood to be cut

and make a mark either side of it to designate its width, which will then become the housing joint. Place a square on the marks and extend the lines across the wood. The marks will need continuing around the corner of the wood to mark the depth of the cut too, but we like to chisel out the long cut marks first so that the edge of the cut is clearer for marking around the edge.

Place the mating piece of wood on the end of the piece the rebate will be cut in. Ensure it is flush with the end, then strike a pencil line across it.

For the housing joint, at the position the joint is required, mark one side of the crosspiece.

Mark the other side to determine the width of the housing.

Extend the line across the wood using a square.

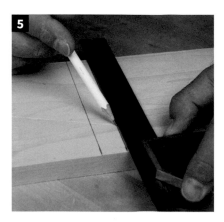

Extend the line the other side of the joint, too.

The next step is to cut the marked lines with a knife to give a sharp edge to the corner of the joint. Continue to do this on all the pencil marks. With a wide, sharp chisel, cut and clear out a small wedge of wood to the cut lines that will create recesses for the saw blade to rest in them. Now continue to mark round the corners and mark a line to set the depth that you want the rebate and/or housing to be. There is no set rule for this depth, but make it at least halfway through the thickness of the wood. Strike diagonal lines to make clear the areas of wood that will be removed.

Cut the pencil lines with a knife to make sure that the joint has sharp corners.

Cut to the knife lines with a sharp chisel to create a recess for the saw blade to run in.

Now mark the lines around the edge of the wood to make clear how deep to cut the joint.

Strike diagonal lines on the waste areas so it is obvious what wood needs to be removed.

Cutting the joints

Position a saw in the recess cut by the chisel and start to saw the cut to depth. Use your finger to steady the blade at first until a reasonable depth of cut is achieved. Continue sawing until the line is reached that determines the depth of the joint. You will probably have to keep an eye on both sides of the wood to make sure the depth of cut is even on both sides. Once the saw cuts have been made, the waste wood can be removed.

The housing joint is a little troublesome as it can only be cleaned out across the grain. Your chisel needs to be narrower than the housing joint and cutting this way is a little time consuming. The process involves tapping the chisel into the end of the wood at the depth of the joint and removing the waste wood that curls out. You may need to turn the chisel over with the bevel side down as you get to the middle so that there is room for your hand to hold the chisel's handle. When the bulk of the waste wood has been removed, it is time for shaving the bottom of the joint so that it is smooth. Take care doing this to ensure that the joint is a good fit.

The rebate is a little easier as there is easy access all across the joint. Position a chisel on the depth line and tap it so chips of wood pop out. Continue doing this across the width of the wood and the rebate will reveal itself, but it will look a bit rough. Using the sharp chisel, gently shave the bottom of the joint until it is nice and smooth and the mating piece fits into it.

Once all the joints have been created they can be fitted together and the item you are building, glued and assembled. Use nails if needed.

Place the saw in the recess cut with the chisel and use a finger to steady the blade until the cut is deep enough to not need it.

Continue sawing until the required depth is reached. Look at the far side to check the cut across the wood.

Use a chisel that is narrower than the width of the housing and place it on the depth line.

Tap the chisel to start removing the waste wood.

Continue to remove the waste wood across the joint. You may need to turn the chisel over so it is bevel down to ensure that there is room to hold the chisel's handle.

Place a chisel on the rebate's depth line on the end of the wood.

Start to remove the waste.

Continue removing the waste across the wood and the rebate will be revealed.

Shave out the bottom of the rebate joint with a sharp chisel to finish the joint.

Finish cutting the joint to depth by shaving slices of wood until the bottom is flat and even.

The finished rebate and housing should look like this.

The rebate allows the crosspiece to fit in it to create a corner joint.

The housing creates a snug fit for a mid crosspiece to fit in.

tips and tricks

FILLING GAPS IN WOODWORKING JOINTS

No matter how good a woodworker you are, there will always be a time when there is a gap in the joint you have created. This is easy to remedy with things you will have to hand. All you need to do is squeeze some glue into the unwanted gap and then rub sawdust from the cuts you have just made into the glued joint. When the glue is dry, lightly sand the joint and the gap will be almost invisible.

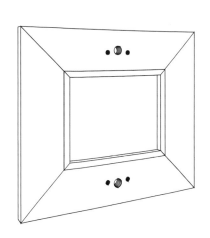

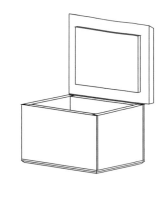

PROJECTS

We have designed and built some attractive and practical items, which can be made using the tools and joints shown in this book. The materials and hardware for these items are inexpensive and easily available. Making them will hone your woodworking skills and encourage you to go on and make more.

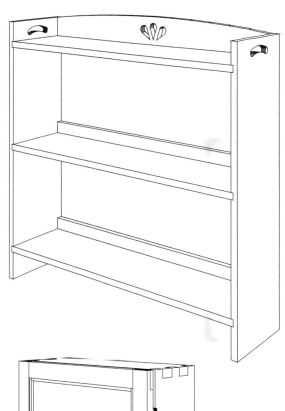

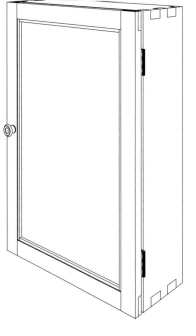

WALL CABINET

This handy cabinet is just the right size for displaying collectibles, a paperback book collection, or family memorabilia.

The unique, interlocking joinery that makes up this wall cabinet creates a strong assembly without fasteners. A little glue is all you need. The box joints (see page 90) add a lot of surface area for glue. They join the four corners of the cabinet assembly. The key to strong joinery is careful layout and cutting to ensure a tight, gap-free fit.

This cabinet doesn't have a back panel, though you could certainly add one if you wish. Instead, we added a pair of hanging rails on the inside that are used to secure the cabinet to the wall. The door frame is made with corner lap joints (see page 74).

An acrylic plastic panel in the door provides visibility for the contents of the cabinet. The cabinet is made from common 1 x 6in (25 x 150mm) wood. The door frame is constructed from 1 x 2in (25 x 50mm) stock. The acrylic panel was purchased from a DIY store and cut to size after the door frame was made.

WHAT YOU NEED

CABINET SIDES
2 @ 24 x 5½ x ¾in
(610 x 140 x 19mm)

CABINET TOP AND BOTTOM
2 @ 16 x 1½ x ¾in
(405 x 38 x 19mm)

HANGING RAILS
2 @ 14½ x 1½ x ¾in
(367 x 38 x 19mm)

SHELVES
2 @ 14¼ x 5½ x ¾in
(361 x 140 x 19mm)

DOOR FRAME STILES (SIDES)
2 @ 24 x 1½ x ¾in
(610 x 38 x 19mm)

**DOOR FRAME STILES
(TOP AND BOTTOM)**
2 @ 16 x 1½ x ¾in
(405 x 38 x 19mm)

GLASS STOP
3 @ 36 x ¼ x ¼in
(915 x 6 x 6mm)

- 1 pair 2 x 1in (50 x 25mm) no-mortise butt hinges with screws
- 1 @ 1in (25mm) cabinet knob
- 1 @ magnetic door catch
- 8 @ shelf pins
- Steel rule
- Marking gauge or combination square
- Knife
- Handsaw
- ¼in (6mm) self-centring drill bit (optional)
- Chisels
- Coping saw
- Hand plane or sandpaper
- Clamps
- Wood glue
- ½in (13mm) or ⅝in (16mm) wire brads
- Straightedge
- Awl
- Double-sided tape
- Wood finish

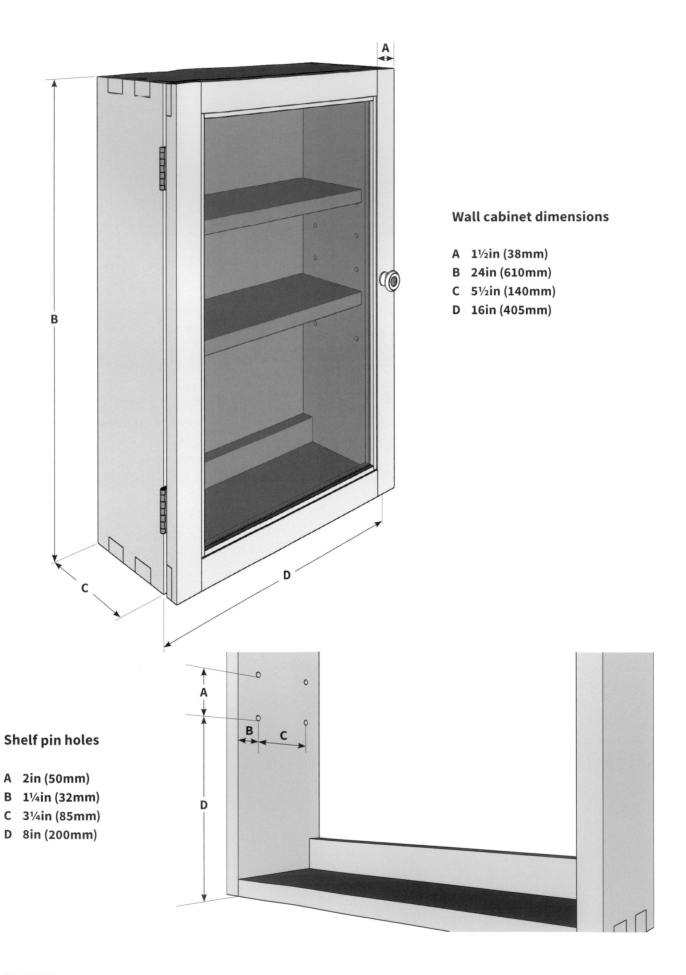

Wall cabinet dimensions

A   1½in (38mm)
B   24in (610mm)
C   5½in (140mm)
D   16in (405mm)

Shelf pin holes

A   2in (50mm)
B   1¼in (32mm)
C   3¼in (85mm)
D   8in (200mm)

Making the cabinet box

The first order of business in making the cabinet is to cut the 1 x 6in (25 x 150mm) stock to final length. The top and bottom are 16in (405mm) long. The sides are 24in (610mm) long. It's important to make sure the ends of the boards are square while cutting them to length. Once the four parts are in hand, take the time to label them with the orientation for the best appearance facing out. It's also a good idea to number the joints at the corners for ease of assembly later.

If you want to allow the shelves in the cabinet to be adjustable, you can go ahead and drill the holes for shelf pins in the cabinet sides. Just make sure you're drilling the face that will end up being on the inside of the cabinet. Shelf pins are available in a few styles and diameters with ¼in (6mm) being the most common. Use the drill bit that matches the pin diameter and drill the holes ½in (13mm) deep.

Laying out the joinery for the box joints at the corners of the cabinet is best done using a steel rule, marking gauge, knife and square. We like to first mark the baseline, or bottom, of the joints on each piece using the marking gauge. For this, we set the marking gauge slightly deeper than the thickness of the workpieces. This allows the pins of the box joints to sit a little proud after assembly. You can sand or plane them flush after the glue dries. Mark both faces and each edge at each end of the four parts.

Lay out the spacing for the pins and notches of the joint on each piece following the dimensions in the illustration. Carefully extend these lines around the end of the workpiece. If you have access to a combination square, this task becomes easier. Otherwise, you can carefully align your square to the previous mark and work your way around.

Now for the tricky part: be sure to properly mark the waste to be removed at each end of the four pieces. Use the illustrations and photos as your guide. The ends of the cabinet top and bottom should be identical. Likewise, the ends of the sides should be identical yet opposite the waste areas in the top and bottom. Careful marking and labelling will help you out here.

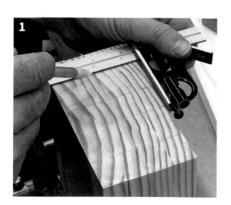

Lay out the box joints for the cabinet sides, top and bottom by stacking them together after cutting them to final length. Use a square to mark the edges of the pins and notches.

Use a knife to score the baseline for the box joints. Trace over the knife line with a sharp pencil to make the line easier to see when cutting. Mark the waste to be removed.

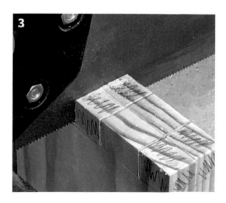

Stack two opposite cabinet sides together (top/bottom and sides) to make the vertical cuts. Keep the saw on the waste side of the lines and cut down to the baseline.

You're ready to make the cuts to create the joinery. Make the vertical cuts first, staying as close to the layout lines as possible without going over. We used a conventional saw for cutting the joint making sure that it had fine teeth for the task of joint cutting. Make each cut down to the baseline you marked earlier without cutting too deep.

You have two ways to remove the bulk of the waste between the pins. You can use a coping saw first then a chisel to pare away the remainder of the waste down to the layout lines. Or you can use a chisel alone, chopping down from the baseline. You'll need to work from both sides of the workpiece to get the cleanest cuts.

The cabinet top and bottom will need to have the waste cut away at the edges of the workpiece.

Use a coping saw or sharp chisel to remove the waste between the pins. If you use a chisel, work from both faces to avoid chipping and tearout on one face.

Begin test-fitting the joints and using a chisel to pare away material until the joint fits tight. Label and work the joints in pairs to make assembly easier later.

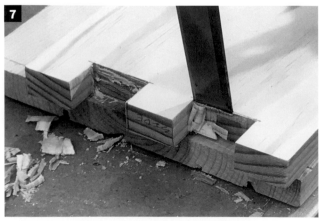

Make sure the notches are cleaned out down to the baseline of the joints to ensure the pieces sit tightly together.

Dry-fit the assembly, check that everything is square, and make any final adjustments to the fit of the joints. Apply glue and clamp together, making sure it remains square while the glue dries.

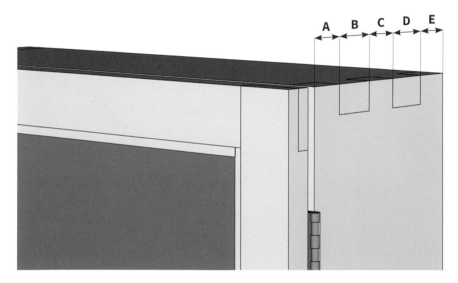

A B C D E

Cabinet joint detail

A   1in (25mm)
B   1¼in (32mm)
C   1in (25mm)
D   1¼in (32mm)
E   1in (25mm)

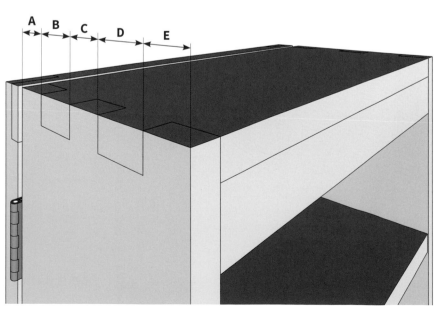

A B C D E

Cabinet joint detail (back)

A   1in (25mm)
B   1¼in (32mm)
C   1in (25mm)
D   1¼in (32mm)
E   1in (25mm)

Once you have all the joinery cut, it's time to test-fit and trim each joint until you get a snug, but not too tight, fit. Work each joint individually and label it before moving onto the next joint. In the end, you should have a box assembly dry-fit with no gaps in the joints. Now is a good time to check that everything is square before you apply the glue. Then you can gently knock the joints apart with a soft-faced mallet, sand the parts, apply glue between the pins of the joints, and reassemble the parts. Measure across the diagonals to ensure the assembly is square before allowing the glue to dry. Apply clamps then move on to adding the hanging rails.

The hanging rails are simply 1 x 2in (25 x 50mm) stock cut to fit between the cabinet sides at the top and bottom. Apply glue along one long edge and clamp them in place flush with the back of the cabinet.

Use a hand plane to plane the pins flush with the cabinet sides. You can sand them flush if you don't have a hand plane. While you're at it, knock off the sharp edges and sand everything smooth.

Now you can make the shelves. The two shelves are made from the same 1 x 6in (25 x 150mm) stock used for the cabinet assembly. All you need to do is cut them to length and sand them smooth.

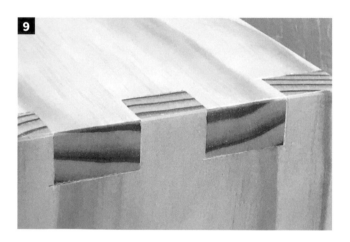

After the glue dries sand or hand plane the joints flush and soften all the sharp edges of the cabinet box using a plane or sandpaper.

Cut the hanging rails to fit between the cabinet sides and glue them in place.

To drill the holes for shelf pins, use a tap 'flag' as a depth stop. Drill the holes ½in (13mm) deep.

After cutting the parts for the door frame to length, stack them as they will be assembled with the edges flush and mark the widths on the adjacent parts. This determines the width of the lap joints.

Stack the four door-frame parts together with one end aligned to score the line with a knife and trace over it with a pencil. Carry this baseline around to the edges of each frame piece.

Making the door

The door frame is constructed with lap joints at the corners. We oriented the joints so that the rails (top and bottom) of the door frame were behind the stiles. Again, a marking gauge comes in handy for laying out the joints. We first made a line that defines the width of the joint. You can use a square for this task. This width matches the width of the mating workpiece.

Use a marking gauge to score the centreline of the lap joint at the end of each frame part. Score a line along each edge down to the baseline. Mark the waste to be removed and verify your cut is on the proper face.

Next, you'll need to mark the depth of the joints. It takes a little trial and error to set the gauge to the exact midline of the thickness of the frame. To do this, make a mark from each face of the frame stock. Then adjust the marking gauge until the two marks overlap at the same spot. Use this setting to mark the depth of the lap joint on the ends of all the pieces.

As before, it pays to label all the pieces and joints as well as mark the waste to be removed from each piece. To make the lines easier to see when sawing, trace over them with a sharp pencil.

Use a rip saw to cut down the midline of the joint. Make sure to stay just on the waste side of the line. Use care at the end of the cut to make sure you don't saw beyond the layout line. Then you can use a crosscut saw to remove the waste. Clean up the joints with a wide chisel or sanding block using your layout lines as a guide, checking the fit often with the mating piece. The goal should be a flush, even fit with no gaps.

When gluing and clamping the door frame, make sure it's square by measuring across the diagonals. After the glue dries, sand everything smooth and knock off the sharp corners with a hand plane or sandpaper.

To hold the acrylic plastic panel in place, we installed glass stop made from ¼ x ¼in (6 x 6mm) strips of wood we picked up at the DIY store. You can also find these at a hobby store. We installed the first set of strips on the inside of the opening flush with the inside of the door. Use small wire brads ½in (13mm) or ⅝in (16mm) long to hold the strips in place. This will also make it easier to remove them in case the panel ever needs to be replaced.

Next, cut the plastic panel about ⅛in (3mm) smaller in size than the opening in the door frame using a series of scoring cuts with a sharp knife. Take your time and use a straightedge to guide the cuts. It will take several cuts to score the plastic deep enough until you can snap it apart. You can file or sand the edges smooth if necessary.

Set the plastic panel in the door frame and cut strips to fit the inside of the frame. For these, we simply added a few small drops of glue and clamped the strips in place.

Use a saw to make the vertical cut down the centreline of the lap joint. Make sure to stay on the waste side of the line.

Make the 'cheek' cut along the baseline to remove the waste.

With the joint cut on two adjacent frame parts, you're ready to test the fit.

Check the fit of the lap joint and use a sanding block, hand plane, or chisel to fine-tune the joint for a gap-free fit.

To easily create a rabbet in the frame opening for the acrylic plastic panel, tack ¼ x ¼in (6 x 6mm) strips of wood in the frame flush with the inside face of the door.

To cut the acrylic panel to size for the door, use a straightedge and make several scoring cuts.

If you've scored deeply enough, the panel should snap in two cleanly and easily at the cut line. If it doesn't do the trick, score the line deeper.

Finishing details

All that's left to complete now is to add a few small finishing details, install the hardware, and add the shelves.

When installing hinges, we like to fasten them to the cabinet first. Lay out the 3in (75mm) distance for each hinge from the top and bottom of the cabinet. Use an awl to mark the centre locations for the screw holes. Use a drill bit just smaller in diameter than the screw threads to pre-drill before installing the screws. A good option is to use a self-centring drill bit. The conical tip on the sleeve automatically centres the internal drill bit in the hole of the hinge.

A trick we use to properly locate the hinges on the door frame is to apply double-sided tape to the loose hinge leaf in the closed position. Then you can set the door in place, ensuring it's centred on the cabinet. Press down on the door frame at the hinges to temporarily attach the hinge leaf to the door. Carefully open the door to mark the screw hole locations as before. Then you can remove the door frame, remove the tape, drill the pilot holes for the screws, and install the screws to fasten the door to the cabinet.

Adding the door knob involves nothing more than drilling a hole and installing the knob with the included screw. Install the magnetic catch at the top or bottom of the cabinet on the inside. Install the magnet base with the magnet flush with the front cabinet edge. Snap the metal door plate onto the magnet with the nibs pointed towards the door. Close the door and press the door frame into the metal plate so the nibs will mark the proper location on the door. Then install the plate on the door with the included flathead screw.

Apply the finish of your choice and hang the cabinet on the wall. It's best to secure the cabinet to a wall stud with screws through the hanging rails.

After marking and drilling the pilot hole for the hinge screw, install one hinge leaf to the cabinet.

Use double-sided tape on the hinge leaf that will be attached to the door. Align the door on the cabinet and press down firmly until the tape grabs.

Carefully open the door and drill the pilot holes. This is a self-centring drill bit to automatically centre them.

25

Install the cabinet knob of your choice by drilling a mounting hole in the door frame.

26

Fit a magnetic catch to keep the door closed. The magnetic base fastens to the inside top or bottom of the cabinet, flush with the front edge.

27

To install the metal plate for the magnetic catch, first place the plate on the magnet with the nibs facing outwards. Press the door frame into the plate to mark its location, then fasten it with the screw.

The finished cabinet

PICTURE FRAME

This is one of the easiest and most popular projects for woodworkers to make. It's an opportunity to show off your skills and your favourite artwork. Our design can be used in either orientation with the holes on the sides or top and bottom.

A basic picture frame is nothing more than four pieces of wood joined to form a frame. For this project, you'll use 45° mitre joints (see page 80) at the corners. They can be tricky to cut and assemble without gaps, but if you follow the steps outlined here and take your time, you'll get good results.

We made our frame from 1 x 4in (25 x 100mm) red oak (*Quercus rubra*) stock from the DIY store. Cutting and fitting the mitres can be a challenge with this wide stock so you may want to practise on narrower 1 x 2in (25 x 50mm) or 1 x 3in (25 x 75mm) stock first. Before you get started you need to determine what size the opening needs to be. These dimensions drive every other measurement for the frame. We used an existing 8 x 10in (200 x 255mm) photo that attached to a 9 x 11in (230 x 280mm) matt frame. The dimensions shown here are for a standard 8 x 10in (200 x 255mm) photograph. If your photo is a different size, you can easily modify the dimensions. If you're upgrading from an old frame, you can use the existing glass as we did. Otherwise, standard photo-size pieces of glass are available at your hardware store.

To create a rebated recess for the glass and photo, we used ½ x ½in (13 x 13mm) strips fastened to the inside of the opening. You can find these strips at the hobby or DIY store.

WHAT YOU NEED

FRAME MATERIAL
1 @ approx. 84 x 3½ x ¾in
(1880 x 90 x 19mm)

WOOD STRIP MATERIAL
1 @ approx. 48 x ½ x ½in
(1220 x 13 x 13mm)

- Sawtooth picture hanger
- Point-setting tool
- Framing points
- Finish nails
- Framing points
- Plastic carpenter's speed square or mitre box
- Combination square
- Handsaw
- Hand plane or sandpaper
- Wood glue
- Power drill
- ⅜in (10mm) and ¾in (19mm) Forstner-style or spade drill bits
- Waxed paper
- Wood finish

Picture frame dimensions

A	17in (430mm)	**F**	10in (255mm)
B	¾in (19mm) dia.	**G**	3½in (90mm)
C	1in (25mm)	**H**	15in (380mm)
D	⅜in (10mm) dia.	**I**	8in (200mm)
E	³⁄₁₆in (5mm)		

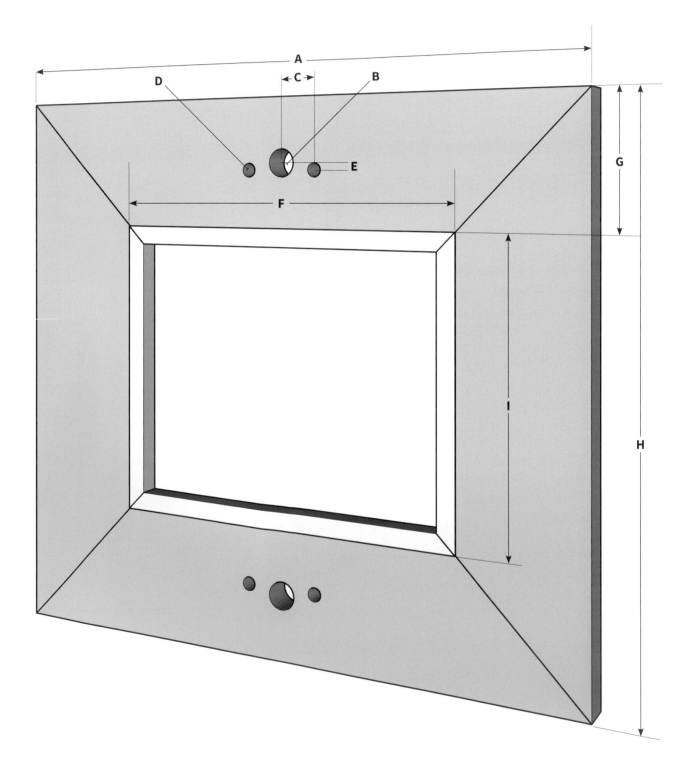

Making the mitred frame

To cut the frame material to size, you can use a mitre box to cut the 45° angles. Another good option is to use a plastic carpenter's speed square clamped to the workpiece to guide the handsaw. To make the four frame parts easier to manage, you can cut them to rough length, extra-long, before mitring the ends.

One of the keys to tight-fitting joinery is for the parts at opposite sides of the frame to be identical in length. And you'll want to make sure that the distance between the 'heels' of the mitres match your photo size. This is the length of the short side of the workpiece after the mitres are cut. In this case, two of the parts will measure 10in (255mm) on the short side while the other two parts measure 8in (200mm) along the short edge.

After the four frame parts are cut, clamp two opposite sides together with one end flush. Clamp them to your workbench so that you can clean up the cut edges with a hand plane. This also makes the parts identical in length. Another benefit is that this gives you an opportunity to make minor corrections in the mitre angle. Use the 45° face of your combination square to check your progress as you plane.

If you don't own a hand plane, you can use coarse-grit (100-grit) sandpaper fastened to a wood block. Be careful you don't round over the edges of the workpieces as you sand. With the pair of parts still clamped together, carefully rotate them to work the mitres at the opposite end. Repeat the process with the other two frame parts.

You can use a plastic carpenter's speed square or a mitre box as a saw guide to cut the mitred 45°-angle frame parts.

With the two opposite parts of the frame clamped together, use a hand plane to trim the ends flush and smooth.

Check the angle of the ends of the frame parts using the 45° face on a combination square. Make minor adjustments with the hand plane.

Now is the time to bring all four parts together and test their fit. First, clear off a flat area of your workbench. Make sure it is clear of dust and debris. Lay out the four frame parts. Mark the joints so that you can keep them properly oriented throughout the process of trial-fitting and assembly.

Use a square on the inside of the frame while you test the fit of each joint. Make note of where the joint is tight and where there is a gap. Plane or sand the high spots on each mating piece and check the fit. As you make progress, the gap will tighten up. Then you can move onto the next joint.

Once you're happy with the fit of all the joints, it's time to glue them up. Cover the workbench with waxed paper to protect it from glue.

Gluing up the frame

With today's modern wood glues it's possible to glue the frame without the use of clamps. Start with one joint. Apply a thin coat of glue to each mating piece and let the glue soak into the end grain for a minute or two. Then apply a second thin coat of glue. Bring the parts together flat on the workbench. Press the parts together while sliding the parts back and forth slightly, ¼ to ½in (6 to 13mm) in each direction, along the glue line until you feel the glue start to grab. When this happens, bring the parts into their final position and hold the joint together for a minute or so. This is called a 'rub joint' due to the rubbing action of the parts increasing the adhesion of the glue.

Now let the glue dry for a couple of hours. Then you can work on the next joint and use the same rub joint technique. Again, you'll need to let the glue dry for a couple of hours. Finally, you can come back and add the fourth frame piece. This is a little trickier since you need to work both joints at the same time. But if the joints are tight to begin with, the glue will do its job. After a couple of hours (overnight is better), you should be able to pick up the frame without it falling apart.

tips and tricks
STRENGHTENING MITRE JOINTS

If you're concerned about the strength of a mitre joint, there's an old trick you can use to reinforce them using wire brads or small finish nails. To avoid splitting the wood as you drive the nail, cut the head off a nail and use it as a bit to drill a pilot hole for the nail. Countersink the nail with a nail punch. Fill the hole with a mixture of sawdust and glue then sand it smooth. Or use a wax crayon to fill the holes after the finish has been applied.

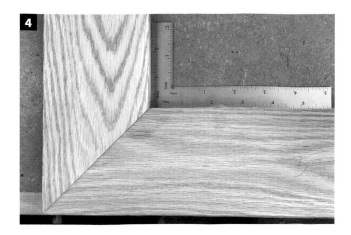

Begin fitting the frame parts together. Fit the joint tight and check that everything is square. Use the hand plane until the joint fits tight and square with no gaps.

After all the joints have been marked and fitted, apply glue to both mating parts of one corner in two layers before assembling the joint.

Once a joint has been glued, let it glue dry for an hour or two before moving to the next joint.

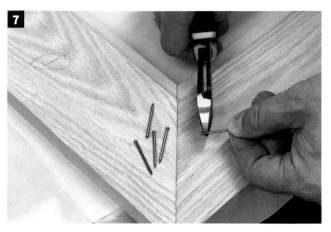

After the frame is glued up and allowed to dry overnight you can reinforce the joints with finish nails to add strength.

Chuck the nail into a drill with the pointed end in the chuck. Use the cut end of the nail to drill holes into the frame.

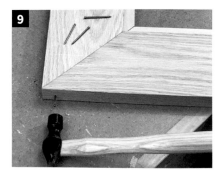

Tap the nails firmly in place leaving them just proud.

Use a nail punch to drive the nail just below the surface.

Frame recess and finish

To create a recess in the back of the frame for the glass and photograph, cut and mitre ½ x ½in (13 x 13mm) wood strips to fit inside the frame opening. We glued these in place about 1/8in (3mm) proud of the front of the frame to add a shadow line for visual interest. Now add the 3/8in (10mm) and 3/4in (19mm) decorative holes, using a power drill. The large hole is placed in the centre of the width of the frame.

If you wish to apply a finish to the frame, now is the time to do so. After the finish dries you can add a hanger and install the glass and photograph or artwork.

You'll need some method to hang the frame on the wall. For this, you can use a sawtooth hanger. Simply centre it on the length of the rail and fasten it with the included nails.

There are a few methods you can use to install the glass, photo, and backer. We chose to use glazier's points and a point-setting tool. These items are inexpensive and easy to use. You can find them at the DIY store. If you're going to be building very many picture frames, you may want to invest in a professional point-setting tool that acts like a staple gun to install the points. If you have difficulty pressing the point into the wood, you can have a professional framing shop do it for you.

Cut and fit the strips that will form the rebate in the back of the frame for the glass and photograph.

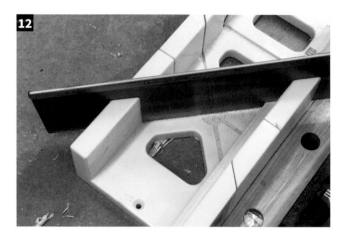

The mitre box is a handy tool to guide the saw when making the 45° cuts on the ends of the strips.

When gluing the strips into the frame opening, leave them proud of the front of the frame to add a shadow line for visual interest.

Drill the decorative holes in the frame. You may want to use a power drill for this task.

Fasten a sawtooth hanger on the back of the frame with two of the included nails. Centre it on the length of the frame.

Use glazier's points and a point-setting tool to secure the glass, photo and backing board in the frame.

The finished picture frame

SHELF UNIT

Offering plenty of space for storing books, displaying photos or family heirlooms, or toys in the playroom, this shelf unit goes a long way to cut down the clutter.

This shelf unit is overall an easy build. Featuring housing joints for a strong assembly (see page 94), it will last for generations. Plus, you can customize the width, height, and depth to suit your needs. We used commonly available 1 x 10in (25 x 255mm) boards for the sides and shelves. You may find it easier to create and fit the housing joinery on narrower 1 x 8in (25 x 200mm) boards. It's a good idea to practise cutting housing joints on scrap pieces first.

To reinforce the shelves in the event they are loaded up with heavy books, and to help prevent items from slipping off the back of the shelves, we added a 1 x 3in (25 x 75mm) lip along the upper back edge of each shelf. The sides of the shelf unit extend above the top shelf. A curved cutout on each side can serve as a handle to move the shelf unit. Finally, the upper back rail is curved with a decorative pattern cut into the centre of the rail.

WHAT YOU NEED

SIDES
2 @ 33¼ x 9¼ x ¾in
(846 x 235 x 19mm)

SHELVES
3 @ 33 x 9¼ x ¾in
(840 x 235 x 19mm)

SHELF LIPS
2 @ 32½ x 2½ x ¾in
(828 x 63 x 19mm)

- Plastic carpenter's speed square
- Marking gauge or combination square
- Knife
- Handsaw
- Coping saw
- Hand plane or sandpaper, rasps and files
- Clamps
- Mallet
- Compass
- Wood glue
- Wood finish

Shelf unit dimensions

A	8½in (215mm)	**D**	13¼in (336mm)	**G**	33¼in (846mm)
B	2½in (63mm)	**E**	3½in (90mm)	**H**	33in (840mm)
C	13¼in (336mm)	**F**	9¼in (235mm)	**I**	32½in (828mm)

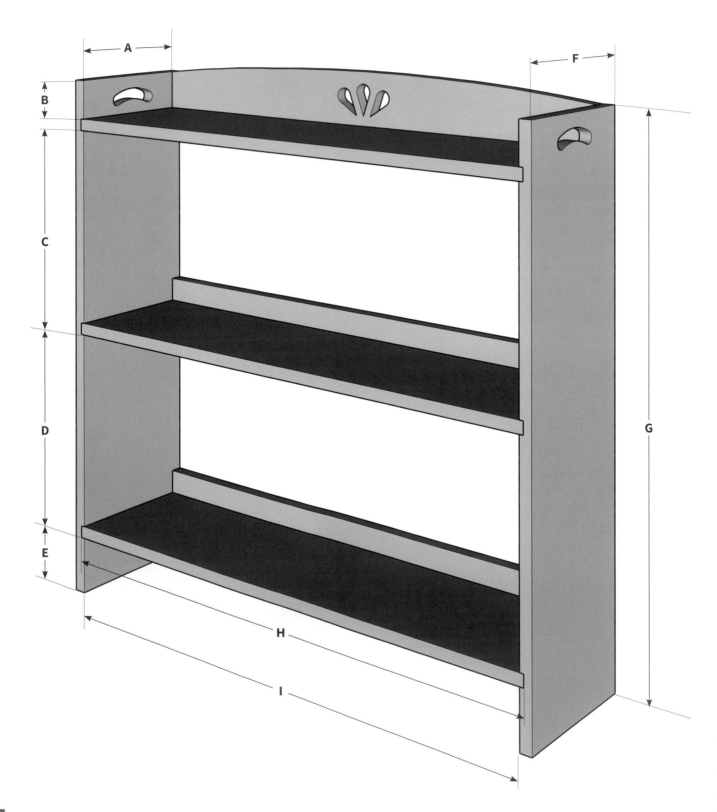

Making the sides

When laying out the parts, play close attention to the appearance of the boards. Use the areas that have the best, most attractive appearance for the top shelf and sides. For consistency, try to cut the sides from the same board. Cut the sides to identical length before measuring and marking out the joinery for the housing joints.

It's a good idea to align the two sides next to each other when marking out the locations for the housing joints. This way, you'll be sure the shelves will be level and square to the sides. To make sure the width of the housing joint is a snug fit with the shelf, use a scrap piece to mark the opposite edge of the housing joint. We like to mark all the housing lines with a pencil, marking the waste area with 'Xs'. Follow up with knife lines. The knife scores the fibres of the wood to create a clean edge when sawing and chiselling away the waste in the housing joint. Before getting out the saw, mark the depth of the housing joint along the edges of the shelf sides. You can use a marking gauge or combination square for this task.

Use a pencil and square to mark one edge of the housing joints in the sides of the shelf unit. Mark the waste area with 'Xs'.

Use a small piece of the material that will be used to make the shelves as a gauge for marking the width of the housing joints.

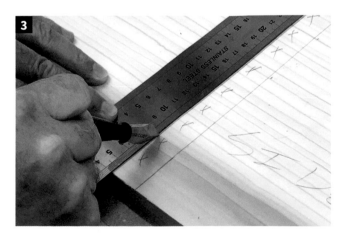

Scribe the edges of the housing joints with a sharp knife to define the walls. Also mark the edges of the workpiece to define the depth of the housing joint.

Clearly marking the width and depth of the housing joints gives you a clear indication of what to remove with the saw and chisel.

Before starting to make saw cuts that define the side walls of the housing joint, we like to make deeper score lines with a chisel along the knife lines. Remove a thin line of chips along the inside of the housing joint to form a track for the saw.

Use your hand saw to cut down each side wall of the housing joint to the depth you marked on the edges of the workpiece. Start slowly and make light strokes to keep the saw cutting straight without jumping away from the line.

Now is the time to get out your sharp chisels to whittle away the waste in the housing joint. Make cuts across the width of the housing joint then tap into the cuts with the bevel of the chisel facing down. Remove chips down the length of the housing joint working carefully to the proper depth. Check your progress frequently using a combination square set to ¼in (6mm). The goal is to have a consistently flat housing joint across the width of the workpiece.

You'll also want to use a scrap piece of shelf material to check the width of the housing joint. For the strongest joint, a snug, but not too tight fit, is best.

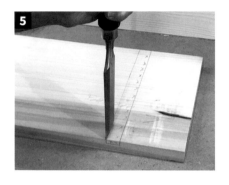

To create a guide for the saw, score the edges of the housing joint a little deeper with a chisel and a few taps with a mallet.

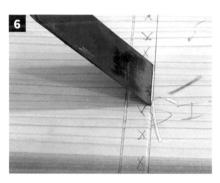

Remove thin chips along the scored edges of the housing joint to form a track for the saw blade.

Carefully saw each housing joint to the depth marked on the edge of the workpiece. Be sure to cut on the waste side of the lines.

Use a chisel to make a series of cuts across the width. Remove the chips, working from one end to the other. Repeat this until you reach the final depth across the workpiece.

Use a cutoff from the shelf material to verify a snug fit in the housing joint.

Arched handholds

Laying out the arched handholes at the top of the side pieces is next. It is a good idea to drill out the holes at the ends of the arch first. This makes for a smoother shape and provides an entry point for the blade of your coping saw to cut out the waste in between. You may want to use a power drill for these ¾in (19mm) holes.

Orient the blade of a coping saw so that the teeth face the handle and so that it cuts on the pull stroke. To remove and install the blade on most older-style coping saws, loosen the handle and squeeze the frame of the saw until the blade releases.

After cutting out the waste of the handholes you can use sandpaper, files or rasps to do the final smoothing and remove saw marks.

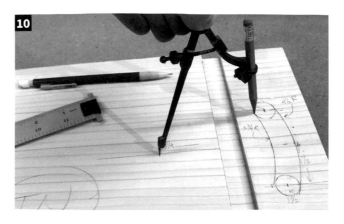

Lay out the shape of the arched handholes using a compass. Drill out the ends before removing the waste with a coping saw.

A coping saw makes quick work out of removing the waste between the holes at the end of the handhole. Remove saw marks with sandpaper, files or rasps.

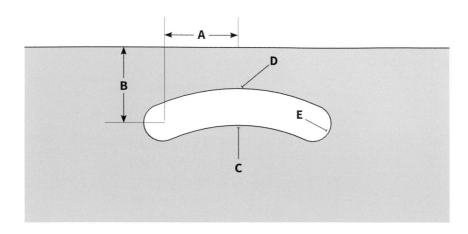

Handhole layout

A   3in (75mm)
B   1½in (38mm)
C   3¼in (85mm) rad.
D   4in (100mm) rad.
E   ¾in (19mm) dia.

Making the shelves

Making the shelves involves nothing more than cutting them to length. Then you're ready to trial-fit the shelves in the housing joints before applying glue. Marking the joints and fine-tuning the fit of each one will go a long way to making the final glue-up easier. Apply the glue in the housing joints, making sure to coat the side walls and bottom of the housing joint. A small, disposable foam brush is ideal for this job.

Apply glue to one side of the shelf unit first and lay it on your worksurface with the housing joints facing up. Gently tap the shelves into place making sure they're fully seated in the housing joints. Then you can apply glue to the housing joints in the opposite side of the shelf unit and tap it into place onto the shelves. Stand the unit upright and apply clamps at the housing joints, making sure the assembly is square as you tighten the clamps. Measuring across the diagonals of the assembly is a good, quick way to check for squareness. The diagonal dimensions should be the same.

While the glue is drying, you can cut the two pieces of 1 x 3in (25 x 75mm) that create the lip on the back edge of the two lower shelves. Take your time to ensure a tight fit, then apply glue and clamp it in place aligned flush with the back edge of the shelf.

Arched top rail

The last piece to add is the arched top rail. For this, cut a length of 1 x 4in (25 x 100mm) wood to fit snugly between the shelf sides at the back of the upper shelf. Mark the ends of the rail at the top of the sides of the shelf unit. These marks serve as guides when laying out the arch on the rail.

To lay out the arch, we clamped a thin piece of wood at the marks made earlier. You can also use a length of ¼in (6mm) dowel rod. Mark the midpoint of the rail at the top edge and use your finger to push the wood strip flush with the top edge of the rail at this midpoint. Trace along the wood strip to lay out the arch.

To remove the waste for the arch, we used a saw from each end and made straight cuts, trying to stay close to the layout line. Then it's a matter of using a sharp hand plane, rasps, files and sandpaper to bring the final shape down to the pencil line creating a smooth arch.

Creating the petal design at the centre of the rail involves a little more layout work, drilling and a few cuts with the coping saw. Take care to make your cuts as straight as possible for the best appearance. Remove saw marks with small files and sandpaper. Finally, go ahead and glue the arched rail in place. After some final sanding, you're ready to apply a finish and put your shelf unit to good use in your home.

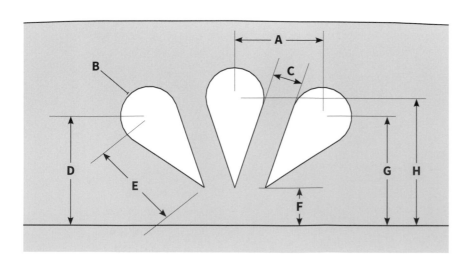

Petal layout dimensions

A 1½in (38mm)
B ¾in (19mm) dia.
C ½in (13mm)
D 1¾in (46mm)
E 1½in (38mm)
F ⅝in (16mm)
G 1¾in (46mm)
H 2¼in (55mm)

After trial-fitting the shelves in the housing joints, add glue and insert the shelves into the housing joints in one of the sides of the shelf unit.

Apply clamps where the shelves fit into the housing joints. The joint should be a tight fit and the shelf assembly needs to be square.

Use a thin strip of wood clamped to the upper rail to lay out the curve at the top of the rail.

Use a handsaw to remove the bulk of the waste to form the arch on the upper rail. Take care to stay on the waste side of your pencil line.

Use a hand plane or a combination of files, rasps, and sanding blocks to smooth out the curve on the upper rail.

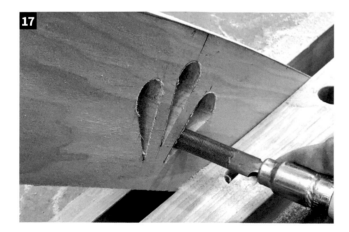

Lay out the pattern in the upper rail and drill the holes. Remove the waste followed by a small rasp to remove saw marks and refine the shapes.

Cut the pair of shelf lips for the lower shelves to fit between the sides of the shelf unit. Glue these and the arched top rail and clamp them in place.

SMALL BOX

Everyone needs a small box for storing jewellery, pocket change, keys or other small items. This box is easy to make with a few simple tools. The bonus is that you can take the opportunity to show off a special piece of wood.

The nice thing about building a small box is that you don't need a lot of material. We used a 36 x 4 x ½in (915 x 100 x 13mm) piece of red oak (*Quercus rubra*) for the box sides. For the bottom of the box, we used 36 x 6 x ¼in (915 x 150 x 6mm) red oak. You can find these small project pieces at a DIY or hobby store.

You can use any species of wood that suits your tastes. For the lid, we used a piece of camphor (*Cinnamomum camphora*), but you can use anything you have available. This is your opportunity to use contrasting or visually appealing woods to make your box really stand out.

WHAT YOU NEED

BOX SIDES
2 @ 5 x 4 x ½in
(125 x 100 x 13mm)

BOX FRONT AND BACK
2 @ 8 x 4 x ½in
(200 x 100 x 13mm)

BOX BOTTOM
1 @ 8 x 5¼ x ¼in
(200 x 135 x 6mm)

- Mitre box or plastic carpenter's speed square
- Marking gauge or combination square
- Knife
- Handsaw
- Hand plane or sandpaper
- Clamps
- Wood glue
- Wood finish

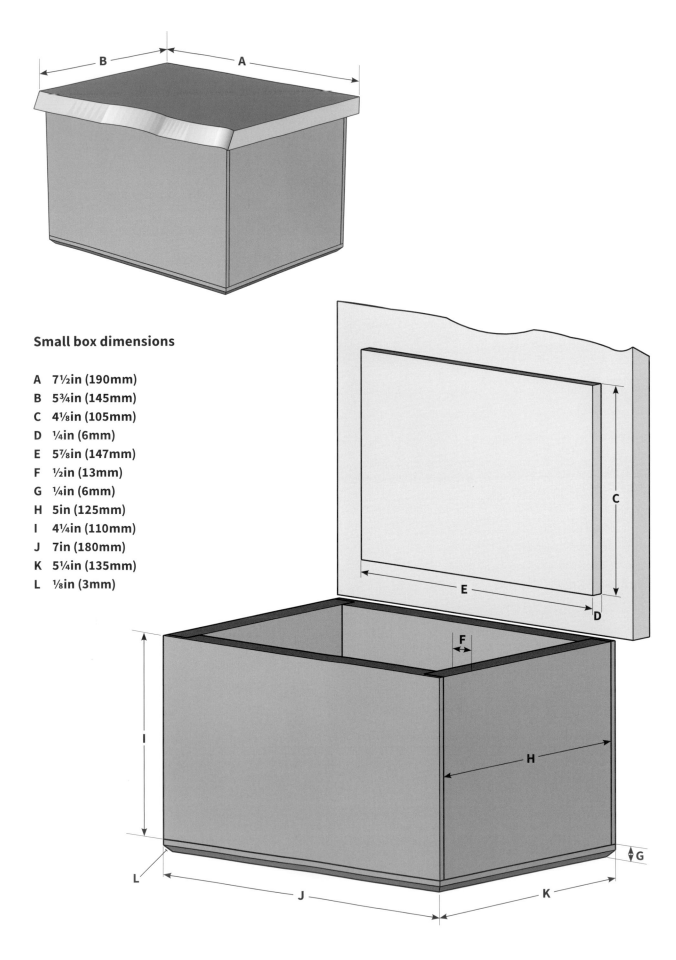

Small box dimensions

- **A** 7½in (190mm)
- **B** 5¾in (145mm)
- **C** 4⅛in (105mm)
- **D** ¼in (6mm)
- **E** 5⅞in (147mm)
- **F** ½in (13mm)
- **G** ¼in (6mm)
- **H** 5in (125mm)
- **I** 4¼in (110mm)
- **J** 7in (180mm)
- **K** 5¼in (135mm)
- **L** ⅛in (3mm)

Making the sides, front and back

To save some time and effort in sawing, we made this box as tall as the width of the wood used to make the sides, front and back. In other words, the box is 4in (100mm) tall, the same width as the ½in (13mm) red oak piece we purchased. If you want to make your box shallower than the width of your workpiece, you'll need to use a handsaw and cut the pieces to width.

To cut the parts to length, you can use one of two methods to guarantee square, accurate cuts. The first option is to use an inexpensive mitre box, which you can purchase at a hardware store. You just need to make sure to hold the workpiece securely as you cut the piece to length. The second option is to use a carpenter's speed square to help make square, straight cuts. Make sure to use a plastic one to avoid damaging the teeth on the saw.

After marking the length of the workpiece to cut, draw a line across the workpiece using a square.

To create a clean edge for the saw to follow, score the cut line with a knife.

Use a mitre box to make a square cut while securely holding the workpiece.

Alternatively you can use a plastic carpenter's square, sometimes called a speed square or quick square.

When cutting a board for the first time, it's always a good idea to cut a bit off the end first to make sure that it's square. Then measure the length of the piece you need and mark the waste side of your pencil mark with a small 'X'. Use a square to mark a line across the workpiece at the mark. Follow up by scoring the cut line with a sharp knife, using a square as a straightedge guide for the knife.

To prevent you from accidentally sawing into the workbench, place a scrap piece of wood on your bench under the workpiece you'll be sawing. Then using either the mitre box or speed square, cut the workpieces to length for the box front, back and sides. Clamp the side pieces together and sand or plane the ends smooth and flush using a sanding block. If you have a sharp hand plane, set it to make very thin cuts to slice through the end grain. Waxing the sole of the plane with candle wax or paraffin will make the plane slide smoothly.

The box corners are joined with rebate joints (see page 94). A rebate joint is nothing more than a notch cut into one piece to accept a mating piece. In our case, the box front and back are notched, or rebated to accept the box sides. Since we're using ½in (132mm) thick stock, the notch needs to be just a hair wider than ½in (13mm). This will leave a little material to trim flush after the box is assembled. The depth of the notch is ³⁄₈in (10mm), leaving only ¹⁄₈in (3mm) of material at the bottom of the notch. This minimizes the end grain showing at the corners, which makes for a more attractive type of box.

To form the notch, it's easiest to score the sides and bottom of the notch on the workpiece using a marking gauge or sharp knife. When using a knife, use an adjustable square to help guide the knife. Mark the waste area with a pencil. Use the speed square or mitre box to align the saw on the waste side of the scored line. Carefully cut down to the line that marks the bottom of the notch, taking it slowly and monitoring your progress as you cut. Once this cut is made, the side wall of the rebate is defined. Make a few more cuts in the waste area and then remove the waste with a chisel. Carefully pare away the waste at the bottom of the rebate, using the scored line as your guide. Test the fit with a sidepiece and continue trimming until the fit is tight.

When all four rebates are cut, dry-assemble the box to check that all the joints are tight. Once you're happy with how it looks, add glue and clamps, checking with a square to make sure the box sides are square.

Use a hand plane or a sanding block to make the ends square and smooth. Be sure not to round over the edges.

Use a marking gauge to score lines on the edges of the notch or rebate on the ends of the front and back pieces.

A combination square can be used as a guide to score a line with a sharp knife.

Score the edge of the notch, then clamp a speed square so the edge aligns with the scored line and cut down to the line marking the bottom of the notch.

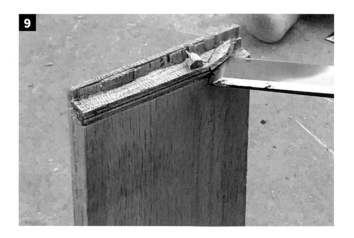

Use a chisel to pop off most of the waste from the notch area. Be careful not to damage the thin remaining material.

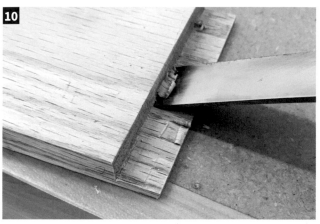

Pare away the waste down to the marked lines forming the bottom of the notch. The goal is a smooth, square notch. Test the fit, aiming for a tight joint.

Once you're happy with the fit of all the pieces, spread a thin layer of glue along both inside edges of the notches.

Clamp across the sides and at each corner front to back to draw the joints tight while the glue dries.

Making the bottom and lid

After the glue dries you can start to work on the bottom and lid of the box. The bottom is nothing more than ¼in (6mm) thick stock cut to fit the bottom of the box. Simply trace the outline of the box and cut just outside the line.

The lid consists of two parts: the main, upper lid and a bottom piece. This bottom piece is also made from the same ¼in (6mm) thick stock. Its job is to position the lid on the box when closed and keep it from sliding off. To make this piece, trace onto the ¼in (6mm) workpiece from inside the box and cut to the lines. Check that this piece fits into the box with just a little wiggle room. Sand all the edges smooth.

At this stage, you can glue the bottom onto the box and sand or plane the edges flush after the glue dries. To make the bottom appear a little thinner, use a hand plane to form a 45° chamfer, or bevel, on all the outside edges of the bottom. You can also accomplish this with a sanding block.

To make the lid, find an attractive piece of wood that is at least ½in (13mm) larger in width and length than the box. This will allow the lid to overhang the box ¼in (6mm) on all sides. Sand the lid smooth before gluing on the ¼in (6mm) piece onto the lid bottom. The only thing to watch here is that this thin piece is centred on the lid. Once the glue is dry, test the fit of the lid on the box. If it's too tight, sand the edges of the ¼in (6mm) piece on the bottom of the lid. After a final sanding to at least 150-grit, the box is ready for a finish. Our preference is an oil and wax finish but you can use whatever suits your style.

Trace around the box onto ¼in (6mm) thick stock to size the bottom and cut it to size, staying just outside the cut lines.

Before gluing on the bottom, trace the inside of the box onto the ¼in (6mm) stock for the lid bottom. This helps hold the lid in place.

After gluing the bottom of the box, sand or plane the edges flush with the box. Create a ⅛in (3mm) chamfer, or bevel, along all of the outside edges of the bottom.

Make the lid about ½in (13mm) larger in width and length than the box. Glue the lid bottom to the underside of the lid, keeping it centred.

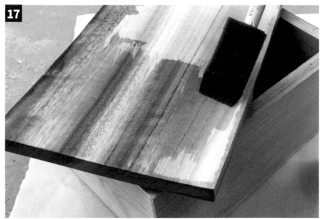

Apply your favourite finish. We prefer an oil finish to make the grain 'pop'. A coat or two of paste wax will give a nice shine.

The finished box

TABLE

This small table is a great exercise in classic woodworking joinery. It will be perfectly at home in your study, den, living room or bedroom.

Made from pine lumber, this table is a good way to gain experience creating mortise and tenon joinery (see page 84). You'll also have the opportunity to cut tapered legs and plane them smooth. And you'll learn that creating a bevelled edge on the tabletop is easier than you might think. Take your time, enjoy the process, and in the end, you'll have a piece that you can be proud of.

The table legs are made from 2 x 2in (50 x 50mm) stock from the DIY store. The table aprons are made from 1 x 3in (25 x 75mm) stock. The top panel is make from a single glued-up panel that we cut down to size.

WHAT YOU NEED

TABLE LEGS
4 @ 17 x 1½ x 1½in
(430 x 38 x 38mm)

SHORT APRONS
2 @ 11¾ x 2½ x ¾in
(299 x 63 x 19mm)

LONG APRONS
2 @ 18 x 2½ x ¾in
(460 x 63 x 19mm)

TOP
1 @ 24 x 15¾ x ¾in
(610 x 399 x 19mm)

CLEATS
4 @ 4 x ¾ x ¾in
(100 x 19 x 19mm)

- Flathead woodscrews:
  8 @ ¼in (6mm)
- Mallet
- Marking gauge or combination square
- Knife
- Handsaw
- Chisels
- Hand plane or sandpaper
- Clamps
- Wood glue
- Wood finish

TABLE **139**

Table dimensions

A 24in (610mm)
B 15¾in (399mm)
C 17in (430mm)
D 6in (150mm)
E 13¾in (349mm)
F 22in (560mm)

Cut all the legs to identical length before laying out the mortises and tapers.

With the legs together, use a square to lay out the top of the tapers and the length of the mortises.

Use a marking gauge or combination square to lay out the ⅜in (10mm) width of the mortises. Mark from opposite faces to keep the mortises centred on the workpiece.

Making the table legs

Cut the four table legs to a length of 17in (430mm). All the legs are identical but some careful layout work is needed to make sure the mortises and tapers are on the proper face of each leg. The tapers and mortises are on two adjacent faces.

Do as much layout work as possible by stacking the parts together. This ensures all the mortises and tapers are aligned. The first layout marks define the location and ends of the mortises and top of the tapers. Flip the legs 90° and repeat the layout marks on the adjacent faces of the legs.

To mark the width of the mortises, use the chisel you'll be using to chop out the mortises as a gauge: in this case, 3/8in (10mm). You can use a marking gauge or combination square to mark from each face of the leg to lay out the 3/8in (10mm)-wide mortises. The mortises should be centred on the width of the leg. We like to score all the layout lines with a knife to create clean edges when chiselling away the waste later.

TABLE **141**

Next lay out the tapers. This can be a little tricky to make sure they end up on the correct face of the leg. The tapers are 6in (150mm) long from the bottom of the leg. Mark lines ½in (13mm) from the face at the bottom end of the leg. This is where the taper starts. Connect this line with the edge of the leg at the 6in (150mm) mark. Mark the waste. Flip the workpiece 90° and repeat the process on the adjacent face. Extend the lines across the bottom end of the leg to the opposite face. In the end, it may look a little confusing but once you complete the layout on one leg, the rest comes easy.

Use a handsaw to remove the bulk of the waste on the tapers. Try not to go beyond the 6in (150mm) layout line for the length of the taper. It's fine if you end up a little short or if there is a ridge of material left; you'll smooth it all out later with a hand plane. If you go beyond the mark, all is not lost. You can simply extend all the tapers to match as you plane them smooth. Now you can clamp a leg to the bench and start planing the taper to the layout lines. It goes pretty quickly with a sharp hand plane. Start working down the high spot and gradually take longer strokes until you remove a shaving the full length of the taper to the layout lines.

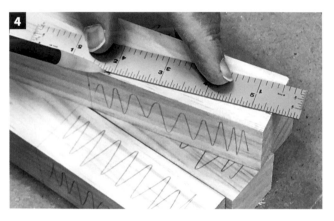

Finish laying out the taper locations by extending the lines to the adjacent faces. Measure ½in (13mm) at the bottom of the leg to define the taper and connect the lines.

After the tapers are all laid out, the workpiece should look similar to this before cutting the tapers.

Use a handsaw to cut down the length of the taper. Try not to go beyond the line marking the start of the taper.

Use a hand plane to refine the taper until it is smooth and straight. Work down the high spots then make longer strokes, working down to the layout lines.

You're now ready to move on to the mortises. One trick you can use is to drill out the bulk of the waste in the mortise first. But these mortises are only ½in (13mm) deep and pine is relatively soft, so removing the waste with a chisel isn't difficult.

Start by using the chisel with a mallet to define the ends of the mortise. You don't need to be timid here – a couple of solid whacks will sever the wood fibres, making the chips easier to remove. Score deeper lines in the sides (cheeks) of the mortises, but take care with this. You don't want to split the wood by driving the chisel too hard. Some gentler taps are in order here.

Once you have scored the perimeter of the mortise, make several cuts across the mortise down its length using a mallet. Then go back and use the mallet and chisel with the bevel down to remove the chips. Repeat the process until you've reached a full ½in (13mm) depth. Use the combination square to check your progress frequently. When cutting the mortises on the adjacent side, you may cut into the previous mortise, which is okay. Your goal is a ½in (13mm) deep mortise with smooth and flat cheeks.

Chopping out the mortises starts with using a mallet and chisel to define the ends of the mortise. Place the chisel with the bevel facing towards the mortise.

Lightly tap the chisel along the cheeks of the mortise. Take care not to tap too hard to avoid splitting the workpiece.

Make several cuts across the width of the mortise. Use the mallet and chisel (with the bevel facing down) to cut and pry out the waste. Repeat to the full depth.

Use a combination square set to ½in (13mm) to check the depth of the mortises as you chisel out the waste.

TABLE **143**

Making the aprons

The four aprons of the table tie the legs together forming a solid base for the table top. The key is snug fitting mortise and tenon joints. So, take your time to aim for a good fit and you may want to consider cutting a practice tenon before cutting all the tenons on the aprons.

The aprons have ⅜in (10mm)-wide x ½in (13mm)-long tenons that fit into the mortises in the legs. The long aprons are 18in (460mm) long and the short aprons are 11¾in (299mm) long. With a ½in (13mm)-long tenon at each end, the assembled table will be 17in (430mm) and 10¾in (274mm) between the table legs.

The first cuts define the shoulders and length of the tenon; a small detail saw works best for this. Make this cut on all four sides of the apron. Next, make the four cuts that define the width and thickness of the tenon. Check the fit in a mortise in one of the legs. It pays to mark the workpieces, always mating the same mortise and tenon as you refine the fit. Use a sanding block or chisel to make adjustments to the tenon for a snug fit in the mortise. When you're happy with the fit, move on to the next joint.

To assemble the table base, treat each pair of legs and the connecting apron as a subassembly. Glue up a pair of legs with a short apron. When the glue dries, you can connect these two assemblies with the long aprons. When clamping, measure across the diagonals to ensure the base is square. The two measurements should be identical.

Cut the aprons to final length, then use a marking gauge to define the shoulders of the tenon on all four faces. Use a square and knife to score the shoulder lines.

Use a mortising gauge or a standard marking gauge to mark the ⅜in (10mm) tenon thickness.

After the tenons and waste areas are marked, you're ready to cut the tenons.

Cut around all four faces to define the shoulders of the tenons.

Make two vertical cuts to define the width of the tenon. Cut just down to the shoulder line.

To finish the tenon, make the two cuts that define the tenon thickness

Test the fit of the tenon in the leg mortise. Label and work each joint individually, paring with a chisel or using a sanding block until you get a snug fit.

Assemble each short apron with a pair of legs to create a subassembly. Pay attention to the orientation of the legs. The tapers will face to the inside of the base.

Join the two leg subassemblies with the longer aprons and clamp them until the glue dries.

Measure across the diagonals to ensure the assembly is square. The measurements should be equal.

TABLE **145**

Adding the tabletop

The large, edge-glued pine panel we found at the DIY store was approximately 16 x 48in (405 x 1220mm). After cutting it to length and planing the ends smooth and straight, lay out the shallow bevel along the edges. It is 1in (25mm) wide by ¼in (6mm) deep.

Clamp the top to the worksurface with the edge of the top overhanging the bench to make it easier to plane the bevel. With a hand plane, begin removing the sharp edge and work your way down to the

layout lines. Rotate the top and repeat the process on all four edges. In the end, you should see a nice, crisp 45° line at the corners where the bevels meet.

To secure the top to the base, we added four small cleats made from scrap ¾ x ¾in (19 x 19mm) material. Cut the cleats 4in (100mm) long and drill a pair of holes for screws used to attach them at the midpoint of the aprons flush with the top edge. But before fastening the cleats to the aprons, drill an oversized hole that will be used to attach the top.

Cut four cleats. Drill mounting holes through one face to mount the cleats to the aprons. Drill an oversized hole to the adjacent face for mounting the table top to the base.

Use flathead woodscrews to attach the cleats to the aprons flush with the top edge. Centre them along the length of the aprons. Orient the cleats so the oversized hole is vertical.

Use your fingers as a guide to scribe a line approximately ¼in (6mm) from the top face of the table top. Mark this line along all four edges.

Use a combination square and pencil to draw a line around the top face of the table top 1in (25mm) from the edges.

This hole is centred in the cleat. The oversized holes allow the top to expand and shrink in width with changes in humidity without the risk of cracking.

Flip the top face down on your bench. Centre the base on the underside of the top and fasten it with screws through the cleats.

Finally, you can sand everything smooth and apply a finish of your choosing.

Clamp the table top to your workbench and use a hand plane to begin forming the bevelled edges. Watch layout lines as you make wider cuts.

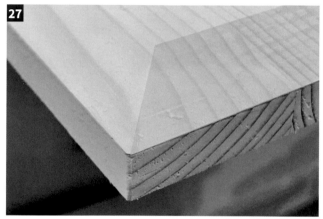

After you've planed the bevels along the four edges of the tabletop, there should be a crisp, 45° line at each corner.

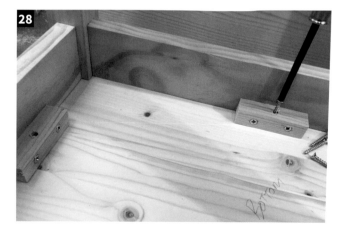

With the tabletop face down on the workbench, use flathead woodscrews through the cleats to fasten the top.

The finished table

TABLE **147**

TOOLBOX

Whether carrying around art supplies, garden tools, or tools for repairs around the house, this toolbox is sure to find a lot of use. With a single pine board and a short length of dowel rod, the construction couldn't be easier.

The toolbox is a simple project to build. It's a great project for younger woodworkers to have a go at too. It's made from a 1 x 10in (25 x 255mm) pine board at least 96in (2440mm) in length from the hardware store. We used simple butt joints (see page 72)assembled with nails. No glue is needed. To create the rounded top on the ends of the toolbox you'll use a coping saw. This will be a good exercise to develop your skills with this tool.

WHAT YOU NEED

BOTTOM
1 @ 17½ x 9¼ x ¾in (443 x 235 x 19mm)

SIDES
2 @ 19 x 9¼ x ¾in (485 x 235 x 19mm)

ENDS
2 @ 16 x 9¼ x ¾in (405 x 235 x 19mm)

HANDLE
1 @ 18¼ x ¾in dia. (466 x 19mm)

- Plastic carpenter's speed square or mitre box
- Combination square
- Handsaw
- Coping saw
- Compass or circle template with 3in (75mm) diameter
- ¾in (19mm) spade or Forstner-style drill bit
- Power drill (optional)
- 4d (4-penny) box nails: 1½in (38mm) long
- Hand plane or sandpaper

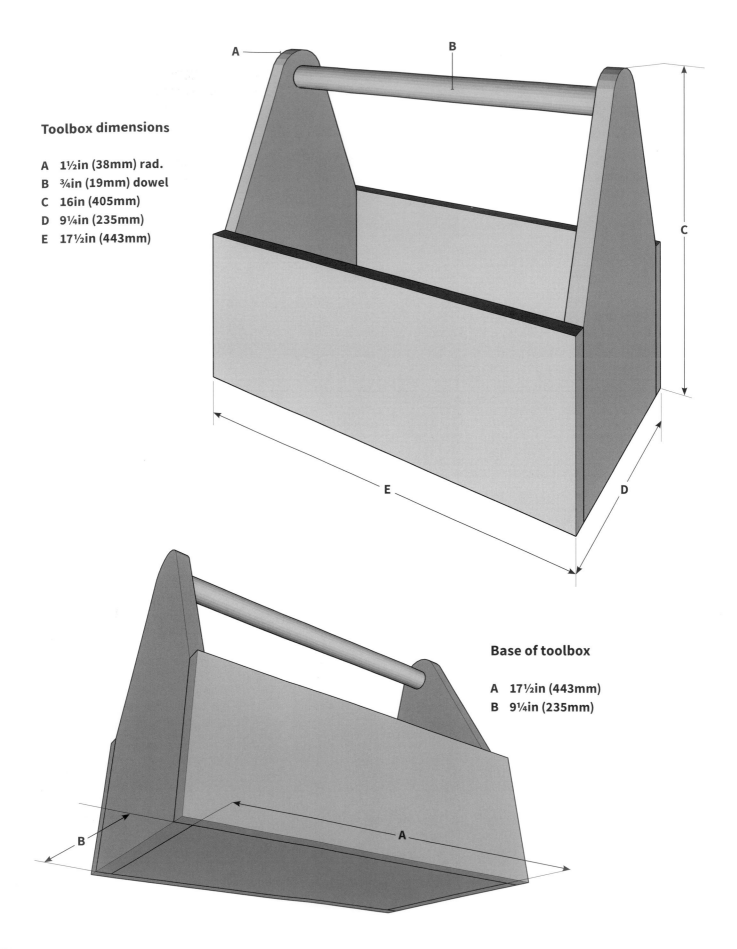

Toolbox dimensions

A 1½in (38mm) rad.
B ¾in (19mm) dowel
C 16in (405mm)
D 9¼in (235mm)
E 17½in (443mm)

Base of toolbox

A 17½in (443mm)
B 9¼in (235mm)

Making the sides, ends and handles

The sides and ends of the toolbox wrap around the bottom, so the bottom is the place to start. Cut it to size with a handsaw. The trick is to make sure the ends are square. You can use a plastic carpenter's speed square to help guide the saw if you have difficulty staying on the line.

Sand the ends to remove saw marks then set the bottom aside while you work on making the ends of the toolbox. These can be cut to 16in (405mm) in length. The ends have straight sides that match the width of the sides 9¼in (235mm) before they taper to a triangular shape at the handle. Make a mark from the bottom edge to indicate where the taper starts.

Get out your compass and lay out a 1½in (38mm) radius at the top centre of each end. Mark the centrepoint with a pencil. Then draw lines tangential to the arc to the 9¼in (235mm) mark you made earlier. This defines the taper of the ends.

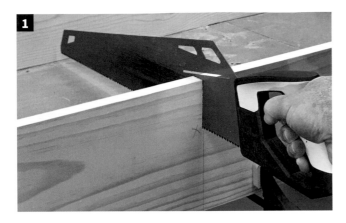

Use a square to mark a cut line. Cut on the waste side of the line.

Use a sanding block or hand plane to remove the saw marks from the cut ends of all the workpieces. This creates a tighter joint during assembly.

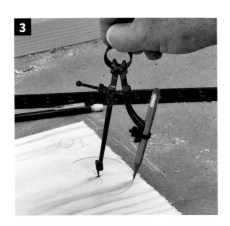

Lay out a 1½in (38mm) radius at the top centre of each toolbox end piece.

Make a mark 9¼in (235mm) from the bottom edge of the toolbox end. Connect this mark to a point tangential to the radius you drew earlier.

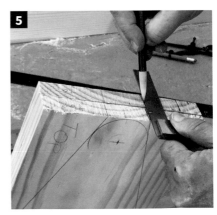

Stack the two end pieces together and use a square to mark the cut line for the taper across the top edge.

Use the handsaw to remove the waste along the taper line. Take care not to cut farther than the layout line at the start of the taper. Use a hand plane or sanding block to smooth the tapers. Next, use the coping saw to cut the curve at the top of each end. You can stack the parts together to do the final shaping with a sanding block.

The last task to do on the end pieces is to drill a stopped hole on the inside face to accept the ¾in (19mm)-diameter dowel handle. The centre of the hole is at the centrepoint of the arc you marked earlier with the compass. Drill the holes ⅜in (10mm) deep. Use a spade bit or a Forstner-style drill bit to drill these holes. You may want to use a power drill for this step.

With the ends complete, all you need to make are the sides and handle. To determine their length, place the end pieces at the ends of the bottom piece and measure the total length. This will be the length of the sides so that they end up flush with the outside face of the ends.

After you cut the sides to length and sand all the pieces, you're almost ready for assembly. The last piece is the handle. Temporarily clamp the sides, ends and bottom together and use a square to make sure the ends are square to the bottom. Measure between the ends then add the depth of the holes to determine the length of the ¾in (19mm) dowel used for the handle. Subtract about ⅛in (3mm) from this total length just to allow a little wiggle room for the handle. Cut the dowel to length and test the fit.

Cut the tapers with a handsaw.

A hand plane makes quick work of removing saw marks and making a perfectly straight taper line.

Use a coping saw to form the radius at the top of each end piece.

Stack the pair of ends together and use coarse sandpaper to refine the shape of the radius. Use fine sandpaper for final smoothing.

Use the centrepoint of the arc to locate and drill the ¾in (19mm) holes ⅜in (10mm) deep on the inside face of each end piece.

To assemble the box

To assemble the toolbox, use 4d (4-penny) box nails. These nails are 1½in (38mm) long. To avoid splitting the wood, it's a good idea to pre-drill holes in the pieces you are fastening. Pick a drill bit that's the same diameter or slightly smaller than the diameter of the nail.

For the best appearance, take some time to lay out the locations for the nails. Aim for consistent spacing and placement. All the nail holes are located ³⁄₈in (10mm) in from the edge.

Pre-drill the nail holes along the bottom edge of the end pieces and fasten them to the bottom, keeping the edges flush. Drive the nails carefully, trying not to mar the workpiece. As the nailhead

contacts the workpiece, give it a couple of light taps to completely seat it without denting the wood. Sometimes it can help to clamp the workpieces together to help secure them as you drive the nails. Remember to insert the handle before attaching the second end.

Now you can pre-drill the nail holes along the ends and bottom edge of the sides and attach them to the bottom and ends. Make sure the ends are flush as you drive the nails.

Use a hand plane or sandpaper to knock down all the sharp edges. Your toolbox is complete and ready to put to use.

Before nailing the parts together, drill pilot holes through the pieces that will be fastened. This helps prevent splitting the wood as the nails are driven.

Align the parts flush and carefully drive the nails, seating them almost flush with the surface. Use clamps to help hold the pieces together.

After the last nail has been driven home, remove the sharp edges with a hand plane or sandpaper.

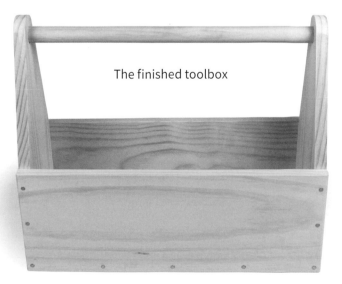

The finished toolbox

GLOSSARY

Arris The term for a sharp edge on wood where two edges meet. It is common to sand this edge to make it less sharp.

Awl Pointed tool used for marking or drilling a small hole.

Bevel An angle on the edge of two meeting surfaces. On a piece of wood a bevel take the sharpness off the edge, on a chisel it allows the chisel to cut in nearer to surface.

Bind Where a saw blade jams in the cut or kerf it has made. This happens when the set of the saw teeth is incorrect.

Bit/cutter A tool used in a spinning action such as a drill bit, a router cutter or a Forstner bit.

Blade The main metal part of a tool. In the case of a saw it is the part that has the teeth, for a hand plane it is the cutter with a sharp edge.

Chuck key A cog-type tool to help tighten the jaws of a chuck onto the shank of a tool.

Chuck A device on a tool, a drill for example, that has teeth that expand and contract to hold the shank of a tool, in the case of a drill it will hold the drill bit.

Clamp/cramp A device with adjustable jaws for holding things.

Claw The forked and curved rear part of the head that is used to remove nails.

Clearance hole A hole that is the outside diameter of the thread part of a screw; it will allow the screw to pass through it.

Dowel Round wood that can be obtained in long lengths. When it is cut short it can be used as a jointing device to fit in matching holes in two pieces of wood to locate their position in relation to each other accurately.

Drill bit A tool for cutting round holes. It comes in a wide variety of sizes and features a spiral flute along their body to assist the removal of waste wood.

Dry fit A term used when checking to see if a joint fits together. It is dry because no glue is applied to the joint.

Dust mask A mask that has pores to allow breathing but which prevents fine dust passing through and into your lungs.

Ear defenders Safety protection for the ears to reduce the noise that can be created by power tools. They can be large over-the-ear types or ear plugs that fit in the ear canal.

Flute A recess feature that runs along the length of a round item. On a drill bit it is a spiral that clears the wood debris when cutting. A flute can also be cut along a round piece of wood as a decorative feature.

Grain The fibrous structure of wood that mostly runs in one direction.

Grit The size of abrasive used on sandpaper or other abrasive equipment such as a sharpening stone. The larger the number, the coarser the abrasive.

Handle The part of a tool that is gripped with the hand to control the tool.

Hone The process of sharpening the cutting edge of a tool.

Jaws The adjustable part of woodworking tools that will close together to hold things between them.

Joint A mechanical device cut into wood to create strength when two or more pieces of wood need to be attached together.

Kerf The cut made by a saw in a piece of wood, its width is determined by the set of the saw.

Metric A unit of measurement used by most of the world. It is a decimal type of measurement with meters, centimeters and millimeters as units.

Nail A small bar of metal with a head and a point, which is hammered into wood to hold pieces together.

Pare Fine cuts made by a chisel where extremely thin shavings are removed by its cutting edge.

Peen The back part of a hammer head. It is available in different shapes, for example, ball peen.

Pilot hole A hole that is the size of the inner diameter of the thread part of a screw. It will allow the thread of the screw to grip in the wood.

Pin/brad A very small nail.

Punch A tool for hitting the head of a nail to recess it below the surface of wood. It has a thin tip and body to hold and a head to hit with a hammer.

Rule/ruler A measuring device that will feature increments in either the metric or imperial system, or both. They can be made of wood, plastic or metal with metal being the preferred option for woodworking.

Safety goggles/glasses Clear goggles and glasses made from a tough material that will prevent debris created by power tools from hitting your eyes.

Sawing The process of cutting wood with a saw. The sharp teeth sever the fibres of the wood and create a cut, or kerf.

Screw A metal rod with a thread and a shaped head. A screwdriver is placed in the head and turned, which makes the thread of the screw pull it into the wood. Screws are used to hold pieces of wood together or attach things to wood.

Seasoning The process of drying wood and removing most of the natural moisture from when the tree is first felled.

Set The angle that a saw's teeth are angled at. A saw's teeth are 'set' at opposite angles on alternate teeth; this gives the saw blade the clearance it needs to cut and not bind in the wood.

Shank The part of a drill bit or any other bit that you insert into a drill, router or other tools that will accept a bit.

Square A tool for measuring and marking right angles. Also a term for expressing that two edges are at 90° to each other.

Teeth/TPI Teeth on a saw are sized by TPI (teeth per inch). The greater the TPI, the finer cut the saw will make.

Thread The spiral feature of bolts and screws that mates with the thread in a bolt or wood to retain the bolt or screw.

Vice A benchtop tool for holding things steady when working on them. It features jaws to hold the item.

Wood filler A type of paste, to repair damage, which comes in many colours so it can be matched to the wood it is applied to. There are other types that can be stained. It is used to fill a hole or crack then sanded flush to the surface.

ABOUT THE AUTHORS

Woodworker and journalist Alan Goodsell has written extensively on woodworking and tools for a range of magazines including the highly acclaimed *Woodturning, The Router, Furniture & Cabinetmaking* (GMC Publications) and *American Router* (Lightning Publications). A significant move took Alan to the USA, where he ran the Marketing Department for a top router bit and cutting tool manufacturer. Still living in Florida, Alan has moved back into publishing and is now producing a range of woodworking-related publications.

Randall Maxey has been woodworking almost since he was old enough to lift a hammer. Born and raised in central Ohio, he owns a custom woodworking business, Cherry Ridge Woodworks. He is also the founder and owner of MiniMaxWorkshop.com, which supports the idea that you can build great projects in small spaces. Randall moved his family to Iowa and worked for ten years as senior editor on a woodworking magazine. He continues to write and edit articles for other woodworking publications and companies. Randall lives with his wife in Florida.

ACKNOWLEDGEMENTS

Special thanks to

Alan's fiancée: Betty Acero
Randall's wife: Sheryl Maxey
Lightning Publications Office Manager: Maria Fernanda Nobregas

INDEX

To order a book, or to request
a catalogue, contact:

GMC Publications Ltd
Castle Place, 166 High
Street, Lewes, East Sussex,
BN7 1XU United Kingdom

Tel: +44 (0)1273 488005
www.gmcbooks.com